Local History Collections:
A Manual for Librarians

Local History Collections

A Manual for Librarians

by Enid T. Thompson

American Association for State and Local History
Nashville, Tennessee

Publication of this book was made possible in part by funds from the sale of the Bicentennial State Histories

Library of Congress Cataloging in Publication Data

Thompson, Enid T
  Local history collections.

  Bibliography: p.
  Includes index.
  1. Libraries—Special collections—Local
history. I. Title.
Z688.L8T48   026'.9788'82   77-28187
ISBN 0-910050-33-3

Printed in the United States of America

Contents

Preface

The city of Englewood, Colorado was once said to have no history. It is a bedroom community, entirely surrounded by Denver and other cities, and is rapidly becoming a city inhabited by elderly persons. Some years before the Centennial–Bicentennial Celebration of 1976 became a reality, the Englewood Public Library undertook a program to identify and establish a record of the history of Englewood, calling it "Share Your Heritage." The people of Englewood responded, and ultimately I was called in as a consultant to develop and organize the program and the collection. As a final stage in this program, the first version of this handbook was produced, funded by a Library Services and Construction Act Title I grant from the Colorado State Library.

Each process, product, and procedure discussed in the handbook was used effectively in the Englewood Public Library Local History Collection. Each can be demonstrated as practical and successful. The collection now is a source of satisfaction to the community, to the library and its librarian, Miss Harriet Lute, and to me.

The interest, the dedication, the enthusiasm of the people of the community in the two or three years I worked with them was a great source of pride and pleasure to me. They shared their homes, memories, mementos, and time generously to document their area. Englewood has a history, now gathered for all to see.

Enid Thornton Thompson

1 Introduction

Local history for its caretakers is much like greatness: some of us are born to it; some of us achieve it by working for it; and some of us find it in the basement in dusty, unlabelled boxes. Whichever way we get it, and whoever we are—librarian, curator, or director of a small historical association—we will have acquired a real treasure for our institutions, especially if we approach our task with some planning and organization.

This book is designed to define the materials of local history and to give very simple advice on how to deal with them. It is not for curators or librarians in large institutions with large budgets and great collections. It is for a group of volunteers starting a local historical society, or a librarian in a public library trying to help people locate the history of their own area, or a museum curator who finds half of the donations to be documentary in nature. It is not designed to be read and remembered. Rather it is written to be consulted as needed: upon receipt of a wrapped package of gift materials, or the opening of a dusty box from downstairs, or at a meeting of enthusiastic but amateur history detectives. The first and most important thing to remember is this: *don't be afraid of local history materials.*

Local history materials do differ from the usual library collection, museum collection, or research collection. They are sometimes hard to find and acquire, to authenticate, to clean, to catalog, to store, and to service. They are of great value and interest to a locality, however, and collecting, processing, and servicing these materials can be very rewarding.

There may be an existing collection to organize

and use, or an organization actively collecting these
local materials. If these resources exist, study the
known history of the area and then take a long,
thoughtful look at the materials in hand. At first
opportunity, read the written material and study the
pictorial material, purely in a spirit of curiosity,
paying no attention to format, condition, or source.
If the material answers questions or sparks a desire
to tell others about what you have found, it probably
has a place in local history. If there is no collection
or organization, start one now.

History is indigenous. Those things that people
have considered important enough to save are the
ones with which to begin a local history collection.
Let this natural selection and grouping process take
its own course and the subjects will clarify themselves. If, during this study, items fall naturally into
groupings such as schools, or people, or decades,
they can be placed together. They can then be left
in these natural subject groupings, perhaps stored
together in files, envelopes, or boxes.

When there are several small boxes or a file
drawer of material, it will be time to decide how
to begin the further organizing of the local history
collection. It may be that some items, such as newspapers or photos or school memorabilia, are already
available in quantity, or are easy to collect. On the
other hand, there may be areas in which no material
is available. Then some work is needed to locate
or create records, perhaps in the form of tape recordings or reminiscences.

This book will provide some helpful ideas about
taking care of what you have, and finding what you
don't have. The detailed information may be ignored
if it is not applicable to your situation or materials.
Guidance into more detailed books and handbooks
is provided for use as the collection and the problems
get larger, both in an Appendix and a Bibliography.

Any or all instructions and advice may be fol-
lowed, adapted, or revised. The specific local situa-

tion will have to direct the development of the collection. Working with local history is in itself a kind of pioneering. Things develop, and adapt, and adjust in this type of collection as they do in history. The end result is usually much more impressive and useful than any of the parts, programs, or processes used in collecting and handling the collection. Like time and history, the building of a local history collection follows the larger pattern of growth and development in an area: it cannot be forced, or hurried, or even very well charted, but danger points and guideposts can be marked. This book is a brief guide to the rewarding business of assembling and servicing a local history collection.

2 Collecting Local History

By the time you need this book, you have gone beyond the question, "Who, me?" or "Who, us?" Either you have a collection to care for, or hope to have one and you want to know how to proceed.

If the community historical society has adequate funding and staff, it probably is the place for the collection. Otherwise, it may be best to use the local public library for this material. These agencies have the interest, the experience, and the overall view of a community. They have the close contact with a large segment of the population on a name-to-name, person-to-person basis.

The collection should be housed in an adequate building with a regular staff. This combination brings order and importance to a local history collection. Whether the local library or the local historical society, the institution needs to be able to adapt its existing services to local history needs. It must define its locale, be realistic in setting limits on its acquisition and service, and define sensible goals. Librarians often know the persons who will contribute to and use the collection, so if the local historical society or museum is not already closely associated with the public library, this association is a good beginning.

Usually this association already exists. Sometimes the organizations occupy parts of the same building, or a museum has moved into the old library building. Perhaps the historical society meets in the library. Regardless of the basis of the relationship, close cooperation often means better collections and better services. And this means better local history.

The institutions should join forces and survey

what they have to work with—personnel, buildings, finances, existing collections. They define the local area—by town, county, neighborhood. Whether library, museum, or local historical society, the first priority is to define the collecting area, the potential support base, and the purpose of the undertaking. The relationship of the institution to the community must be explored before collecting begins.

The task then becomes one of laying a foundation of fact, providing illustration and illumination of fact, putting the area and its incidental history in context, and providing perspective. The tools which the society needs fall roughly into these categories:

Books
Pamphlets
Newspapers
Periodicals—periodical articles
Photographs and prints
Tape recordings
Ephemera
Clippings
Manuscript materials
Memorabilia
Maps and measured drawings.
"Collections" and such items as scrapbooks.

A local history collection in a public library building.

Once an institution has publicized an interest in collecting these things, they begin to arrive as gifts. Here is a use for the material in those dusty boxes in the basement.

Once the decision has been made and publicized to start or add to a local history collection, availability of materials must not be the only criterion for collection. Different kinds of materials have different value in potential usage and in cost of processing and upkeep, even if the only cost is staff time and labor. Storage space is also a prime consideration in accepting materials. So while everything can be considered acceptable at first, some things are more valuable than others, and should be so judged.

Usually photographs and newspapers are the most valuable items for a small institution to collect in depth. Such sources are used a great deal in research and publication; providing them makes friends for the institution that owns them. They attract public- ity—and other gifts. Ephemera is often of marginal research value while a collection is small, but it can illuminate other materials in a larger collection. Manuscripts, maps, and tape recordings are usually rather difficult and expensive to acquire, process, store, and service. However, if they are available they can become very important to a collection.

In the preliminary survey of the materials in local history, the resources of the community to extend the usefulness of the collection should have been noted. These include people who have knowledge of local events and those who own relevant books or other materials. The expressed needs of the com- munity for local history must be considered: at what grade is the history of your state taught in your school system? What is the history taught with— slides, texts, films, or personal visits to museums? Is there need for special materials in the high school, or the college curriculum? After studying the needs of the community, decide which materials will pro- vide the most local history for the amount of time, money, and energy available. Base your collection on need, already existing materials, and the chosen kinds of materials. Work on collecting these items, but do not close your mind to accepting other kinds. The situation may change unexpectedly; someone may offer an entire ninety-year collection of local photographs, for instance, while you are searching for newspapers. So be prepared for the collection to expand to all the types of materials, or to greater depth and more documentation.

Until and unless these changes occur, however, plan to expend your energy and funds in building the most useful collection for your own situation. While there is always interest in local history, lack of space and staff means that value judgments must be made about collecting, processing, and servicing. It is far better to have a well-balanced, well-managed, well-used collection of bound newspapers and photographs in a small area than several hundred boxes of unidentified, unprocessed, unuseable miscellany stored wherever there is space.

These local history materials are going to be studied; this means that a research or reference-type situation must be provided, staffed, and serviced. The library, museum, and historical society are all going to find themselves facing the same demands. The library has more experience in these areas, and so its techniques are a good place to start in organizing and processing the materials of local history.

3 The Materials of Local History

The materials of local history differ from traditional library materials, and are handled somewhat differently, but the traditional functions of acquisition, processing, and servicing are basic to both. Often documentary materials show up in the collections of museums or historical societies; these institutions attempt to accession, catalog, and exhibit their materials. To these traditional tasks the historical society had added dissemination of local history with education programs, publishing, and lecture activities. Whichever institution is handling the collection of local history, the processes are the same, and so is the beginning point. Any local history collection is going to be based on books.

Books

In an established institution, a special collection on local history is added to a carefully gathered collection of books about the state and region, a file of local newspapers and periodicals, a well-guarded collection of books by "local" authors, and specialized books about the immediate area. These books and periodicals usually cover a geographical area larger than the defined community, since the larger area is usually the subject of the books. There are also many textbooks for use of students of the state's history, which is a required subject for students in most states. This book collection, particularly if it contains early books, is traditionally kept in a locked case, and is used only in the institution. Most

A locked case is the best way to prevent the theft of rare or valuable books.

libraries make a practice of buying at least two copies of books on local subjects, one of which circulates, and one of which is locked up immediately. This list includes histories and regional or local travel books, as well as works by local authors and biographies.

The books to be acquired as the basis for a local history collection, if no other exists, include:

> Standard state and regional histories—as many as possible;
> The old and the new texts for teaching state and county history;
> Copies of both adult and children's books about life in the area;
> Travel and recreational guide books;
> Biographies;
> Directories;
> Fiction and nonfiction.

Genealogical materials as such are not of great value in a local history collection. Emphasis should be placed on the historical development of the area. This of necessity means histories of persons, families, and businesses and the part they played in development of the area. It does not mean a primary concern with family trees and relationships except where this point is important to the history of the area. However, much genealogical research will be done in a local history collection.

Directories of all kinds are especially helpful—city directories, business directories, school rosters, club rosters, church rosters, and telephone books. When the current edition of such a directory is superseded, the old one should be added to the series in the locked case.

Books and periodicals are always best handled by regular book and periodical cataloging and control systems used in a library setting. The books describing these library services are listed under "Technical Processes" in the Bibliography. Your local library or historical society should be the first place you

Early and more recent city directories. These are valuable local research aids.

go to get the books and articles listed in all sections
of the Bibliography. These agencies use technical
control and cataloging systems, and usually they
have the technical books on hand. If important titles
are lacking, they can find them.

There is a fairly new library activity known as
"networking". This is a federal- and state-funded
library system that allows requests for information
from even the smallest library to be answered from
the resources of the largest—such as state university
or large city collections. The network can usually
make journal articles available to the small institutions. By securing and keeping copies of these articles, a historical collection can build a good
"how-to" collection for its use, at a very minimal
cost. Books and technical leaflets from the American
Association for State and Local History and the
National Park Service can be obtained at reasonable
prices. Acquisition of material that cannot be borrowed or copied should be discussed with your
librarian or society resource person. He or she can
tell you about discounts, special sources, and other
buying helps available to educational institutions.

Books and periodicals from the local history collection are noncirculating and are checked for damage after use more closely than normal books. It is
necessary to suspend some book collection criteria
to include books by local authors or with local
settings—local interest taking precedence over quality. It is also necessary to be particularly careful
about the binding or rebinding of local history materials. An old history book cannot be rebound by the
usual commercial binder, who cuts margins, replaces
end sheets, and trims edges. They are better boxed
and used in a delapidated condition than bound
badly. The same is true of periodicals; bad binding
jobs are irreversible, and destroy the integrity of the
book or periodical.

Pamphlets

Pamphlets published in or about the area are valuable items in a local history collection: Chamber of Commerce brochures, the land pamphlets published by the railroads in the settlement period, advertisements for stores and theatres, catalogs of local merchants or farms or ranches, catalogs of schools and academies—all contain information. If there is serious factual error (and sometimes there is, particularly in a promotional item), the errors should be noted in soft pencil on the item, with the authority for the correction given. For example, on a pamphlet promoting a ski area, if the area was never built because of lack of snow or lack of funding, the newspaper accounts of the affair can be cited "SEE *The Echo* Mar. 11, 1966, p.4" or "John Jones, promoter, told Mrs. Jim Smith that the company folded for lack of money in March, 1966." The maps, the photographs, the names and the dreams shown will nevertheless have contributed something valuable to the local picture.

Pamphlets should be saved and protected with some type of cover. The two pamphlets on the right are wrapped and labelled.

Pamphlets should be placed in the protective cardboard or plastic covers usually used in libraries, provided they can be used without damaging the pamphlets. It is probably better to place them in good quality Markilo envelopes or acid-free binders. (University Products Inc. has an acid-free board pamphlet binder. Addresses for suppliers of archival quality products are given in the Appendix. Write for catalogs.) Placed in envelopes, the pamphlets can be included in the ephemera file; in covers, they can be cataloged as monographs, and placed on the shelf with the books. File-size and acid-free envelopes or document boxes or cases can hold a number of pamphlets on closely related subjects. The photographs in pamphlets are often not available anywhere else, and are therefore valuable for historical study. But since they are usually printed by a halftone or screening process, they are not good for reproduction.

Newspapers

The real backbone of any purely local history collection is a file of local newspapers, either original or on microfilm. If an institution does not own such a file, this should be its first acquisition. To go about this, first thoroughly explore the possibility of the existence of a file elsewhere in the area. Publishers are required to maintain files, but often, since they do not wish the responsibility of providing reference service, they donate the files to a public institution which will. Or they may loan their holdings for microfilming, which means that reference service is readily available, and the information is protected by having copies in more than one place. Microfilm does involve some expense, both for filming and buying a reader, but it is an excellent tool for both research and conservation.

A complete file of local newspapers is the most important holding in a local history collection.

Reference tools for locating files of newspapers or microfilm exist. They list holdings, where copies may be purchased, and other details. Two national ones that list newspapers are:

> *Ayer Directory of Publications*
> Ayer Press, 210 West Washington Square
> Philadelphia, Pa. 19106

and

> *Newspapers on Microform, United States,*
> *1948–1972*
> Library of Congress, Washington, D.C. 20006.

The Ayer *Directory* is usually found in reference libraries, and it lists current newspapers by state and town. It also lists county names and related local information. *Newspapers on Microform* uses the same state and local approach. Old issues of Ayer's show up in many newspaper offices or libraries, and contain much valuable information about early newspapers for a locality. So do old city and state directories.

Another general reference tool that is useful in looking for files of newspapers or periodicals is

Ulrich's International Periodicals Directory
R. R. Bowker Co.
1180 Avenue of the Americas
New York, N.Y. 10036.

This directory uses a subject approach, and would be helpful in locating periodicals of interest to a special area, under such headings as "agriculture", "travel" or so on.

The state library or state historical society usually holds a large collection of state newspapers, and most have microfilm copies. This means that positive copies for research and reference are relatively inexpensive, because a negative has already been made. In many states, positive copies of almost all older newspapers in the state are available from the state historical society. If an outlying institution has available a file of newspapers not already on film, the historical society will probably make their experience and expertise available to get the file on film, which is a great help for a new institution borrowing the papers to copy.

Bound volumes of older newspapers take up a great deal of space.

State historical societies have made a practice of listing not only newspaper holdings, but also newspapers that have been published for which no files are known to exist. They usually have these lists published, with a great deal of extra information—such as dates, editors, publishers, and name changes.

Bound volumes of newspapers are terribly bulky, hard to handle and service. Many persons would rather work with an original file of newspapers than with microfilm, but as an alternative, microfilm cannot be overlooked. It makes possible the copying of items that would not otherwise be available; it reduces the dangers of loss due to wear and mutilation. Microfilm is easier to service, it can be used to make copies, and it is readily obtainable. It also aids in the conservation of the originals. But microfilm's greatest benefit to local historical societies is in enabling them to build and service a good file of local newspapers.

Large volumes are difficult to use, especially in the limited space of the archives.

Provisions should be made to collect current local papers as they appear. If space is a problem, they should be discarded as soon as microfilm is available, or clipped for the ephemera file. Care should also be taken to collect files of advertising newspapers that are distributed free in a community. Several copies of special issues of the local paper, such as anniversary or holiday issues, should be secured to place in the ephemera file as well as the newspaper file. Constantly increasing costs of publication and postage make it more difficult now to get a free subscription from a publisher of a local paper, but even if a subscription has to be paid for, or the paper picked up in person, a file of local newspapers is still the most important part of a local history collection.

Periodicals

Magazines or journals published in a locale or dealing with it should be acquired, whether they are literary, business, advertising, or anything else. The publications of the state university, state historical society, local colleges and schools, and other groups should be collected.

Magazines of special interest in the area such as skiing magazines, mining journals, farming journals—anything that is apt to mention the locale or the area—should also be subscribed to or acquired from people who subscribe. If the issues are not of enough interest to justify storage space, they should be clipped for articles of local interest. The articles may be dropped into the ephemera file after the name of the magazine and the date are noted on the article.

A periodicals collection includes bound and unbound issues of local interest.

A study of *Ulrich's Periodical Directory* or the serials list or periodicals list of the state university will give an idea of some of the periodicals published in the state both current and defunct, so that it is possible to recognize these pertinent publications.

Photographs and Prints

Materials in a picture collection can be of several kinds: photographic prints, film negatives, glass plate negatives, glass or film slides, clippings, picture books, post cards, albums, lithographic or other kinds of prints, sketches, and paintings. Photographs are usually the easiest of local history materials to collect. Almost every family has photos of people and events of the past, since amateurs with cameras have been common since the late nineteenth century. Every town had its professional photographer, or one who visited on schedule. Prints or negatives of these pictures are often still in the possession of the photographer or his family. The photographer or his heirs may be persuaded to donate the collection for the prestige it will bring the society and the photographer.

If the owner will not give the pictures outright, he will often loan the original prints, or better yet, the original negatives for copying. The most important task after acquisition of pictures is securing identification from the donors of the persons and places depicted, and establishing the history of the photo itself: who took it, where and when, and sometimes why.

In small collections, all graphic material is handled in the same way. Photographs, prints, and drawings can be easily and safely copied by photographic means, thus sparing the originals. Making copy negatives and copy prints for the pictorial file is well worth the effort and expense. Some photocopiers make prints sharp and detailed enough to be used as reference prints. No one is surprised to find photographic clippings or post cards in a photo file, and scrapbooks or photo albums are gradually incorporated by making copy negatives and prints.

Whenever possible, acquire both negative and original print. It is much easier to get a good sharp print and to bring out details of a photo from an original negative than a copy negative, so the quality

Picture postcards are great sources of local information.

of a collection improves in direct ratio to the number
of original negatives in it. Each photographic process
used in copying an image causes about a ten percent
loss of detail and sharpness. While copy prints or
photocopies are usually used for study and handling,
original prints are important as historical artifacts
and are specially protected. Valuable slides are handled by themselves but in related ways, because they
add depth to a photographic collection, and because
they are so easily available.

Photo and negatives come into a collection in
various sizes. If prints are borrowed to be copied,
or a collection of negatives is being built, a size for
each must be decided upon. Negatives reproduce
well and are least expensive in the 4″ x 5″ size. Prints
ordinarily come in 4″ x 5″, 5″ x 7″, or 8″ x 10″ sizes.
In deciding upon a size for prints, the 5″ x 7″ print
has the advantages of optimum clarity with econ-
omy; there is considerable loss of detail in a 4″ x
5″ print, and 8″ x 10″ prints are expensive. Prints
should never be ordered without margins.

Prints, whether copy or original or both, and the
negatives that go with them should be kept together
until the negatives are numbered and identification
is noted on all the parts of the set. Ball point pens
filled with india ink are now available for marking
negatives. Only a soft (no. 2) pencil is used to write
on the back of a print, and then the writing should
be confined to the edges of the print if possible.
Never write on the face of a print, and be very chary
of writing on the backs of original prints except
around the edges. In spite of the newspaper practice
of pasting captions or typed slips on the bottom or
back of prints, this should not be done in a historic
collection. Captions can loosen or rip off, thus damaging both prints and identifications.

Identification for a photo should include names,
places, dates, details, name of photographer, name
of donor, and any other facts that can be found.
If there are differences of opinion, these should be
fully recorded.

The back of a copy print, or the identification note for an original print or negative should look like this:

Englewood 1920–29	*Subject heading*
Broadway 3400 block Looking north ca. 1924	*Identification*
Taken during Englewood Days Celebration by John Doe	*Photographer*
Gift, 1972 from Pearl White J. Doe's granddaughter	*Donor*
Neg. #111 Slide #23	*Neg. no. Slide no.*

The negative number, assigned to each negative in numerical succession by the person in charge of the collection, is placed on all parts of the set of photographs—original print, negative, and any copy prints and negatives. One master list of negative numbers is kept in the collection. An original print or a copy print without a negative number means that there is no negative of the photo in the collection. If one is made in response to a need for a copy print or as a means of protecting the original, all copies of the photo must be identified by the new negative number. This number should be placed:

1. In the lower left-hand corner of the negative on the non-emulsion (shiny) side with the india ink marker.

2. On the outside of the negative envelope, along with the rest of the identification of the photo.

3. In the lower left hand corner of the back of the print. This number is placed even on glass plate negatives, along with the original photographer's number. This is the only mark ever used on glass plates. The original number is also noted in the identification of the prints, usually prefaced by the name or the initial of the photographer.

If a print is made from a slide, or if a slide has been made from a photo, the slide number should also be noted on the back of the print, although slide numbers and negative numbers are not in the same numerical sequence. A slide number is placed on the lower right edge of the print, as shown in the illustration. *The negative or slide number is the only key between the negatives and prints or slides.*

The negatives are filed in numerical order, each in a small acid-free envelope or acetate Kodak sleeve placed in a manila envelope. All information about the negative must be written on typed on the envelope, and constant vigilance must be used to make sure the number on the negative and the envelope correspond.

Original prints should be sleeved individually—Kodak sleeves, mylar, or triacetate are recommended—and placed in acid-free envelopes or folders. Ideally, photo files should be kept in acid-free document boxes and put in metal filing cabinets or on metal shelving. Original prints are either filed by subject in an "original photo" file, or are sleeved with identification and filed in the regular subject files, in groups of ten to twenty-five.

The subject headings under which the prints are filed are the same ones used in the rest of the local history collection, and also grow out of the collection itself. Establishing these headings is discussed under "processing." A set of instructions for working with photos appears in the section on volunteers, p. 67.

Archival storage of photographs. Acid-free boxes containing photo files rest on metal shelving. The light source is shielded.

This system of organizing pictures is self-indexing due to the use of subject headings, which are assigned by the curator of the collection. If the number of prints kept in an envelope is predetermined, it is easy to collate photos after use by counting or by checking the subject heading that appears on the upper left-hand corner of the print with that on the envelope. An ideal situation is one in which only copy prints are used in the study files; if this is not possible and the originals are used, they should be protected by a sleeve. Prints can be used for study without a negative, but negatives must never be filed without a print for reference.

Any number of prints or negatives can be added to the collection at any time; this simple self-indexing system is open ended, and the numbering system serves as an inventory control. The counting of prints into a folder protects against loss. Prints can be added to the study collection without a negative, but negatives must be printed before they are useful. If large negative or glass plate collections come in without prints, they should either be printed or kept together by the photographer's name until such time as they can be printed.

Slides, whether glass lantern slides or modern 2½" x 2½" filmslides, are numbered in sequence as they are acquired and are filed in numerical order. Notes of slides and slide number are made on the corresponding print if one exists, which again is used as the reference key. If a slide exists for which there is not a print, an index card should be made with all the information about the slide, including slide number and/or negative number. This card is dropped into the subject folder or envelope of prints so that a curator or researcher will realize that the slide exists and can be seen or used.

A researcher looks through a file of well-protected photographs.

Film slides may be stored in various ways. Sectioned sleeves that take several slides may be purchased and placed in notebooks, or regular slide boxes may be purchased from photographic stores. It is essential to keep slides in numerical order and accessible as well as protected from dirt and light.

Supplies for the processing and storage of prints and negatives are not hard to find. Regular manila file folders will do for storage in file cases, or in Hollinger boxes. Acid-free photo envelopes and folders are available from library supply houses or such companies as TALAS or Hollinger. Addresses of these suppliers are listed in the Appendix.

A book published by the American Association for State and Local History, *Collection, Use, and Care of Historical Photographs*, by Robert A. Wein-

stein and Larry Booth, is an invaluable aid in learn-
ing about and dealing with pictures. It should be
consulted early, often, and thoughtfully by anyone
interested in working with pictures in a collection.

Also, when working with a photo collection, the
assistance, advice, and moral support of the local
photographer or photographers is important. A photographer who runs his own shop and does his own
processing of negatives and prints can answer questions that may arise about printing and processing
photos for maximum detail and long-term stability.
They can often improve the quality of poor prints
with good copying methods. They are often willing
to help secure materials for the best possible price,
and they often hear of important local material that
could be added to the collection. A local photographer may also donate his photo collection,
knowing that local history is preserved, and well
preserved. As in any adventure into local history,
local people and local interest are essential.

Tape Recordings

One of the more recent and successful methods
for collecting local history is tape recordings. The
inclusion of oral history tapes in a collection greatly
expands and enhances an entire collection. It ex-
plains pieces of memorabilia; it fills in details of
episodes; it gives differing viewpoints; and it brings
an entirely human dimension to facts of history. So
much excellent material on the development and
methodology of oral history been written in the last
few years that this discussion will be rudimentary.
The tape recording is a tool of history, and should
be used as a tool—as a means to an end, and not
an end in itself.

Tapes are made either on cassettes or on tape reels.
The cassettes and cassette recorders are small and
easy to use, while the reel tapes and machines are
harder to handle. The cassette recorders are usually
not as expensive as the big reel machines, but the

cassette tapes are more expensive than reels. Since it is fairly easy to erase a recording while using it, do not let the original tape be played. Make a copy of the original or master tape for reference, and store the original. It should be stored in a wooden case, as metal cases produce magnetic reactions in tape that can destroy sound quality.

After the acquisition of a recorder and some tapes, the next problem to be faced is selection of the interviewer and the interviewee. The interviewer must be familiar enough with the history of the area so that he can keep the conversation going unobtrusively and yet does not overlook important leads. Storytellers sometimes are so familiar with their material that they leave out important details. Often memory plays tricks on the interviewee; the interviewer should be knowledgeable enough to introduce discussion of the facts as they are recorded elsewhere. The basic written materials in the local history collection should be firmly in the interviewer's mind as an outline on which to record oral history. The interviewee must have a good knowledge of the subject on which he is speaking, and should be selected to fill gaps in local history, such as details about churches or business or special subjects. Often having two or more persons interviewed at the same time makes an interesting tape, because one person's recollections stir another's. Persons who have been active in the community should be asked about their contributions, and officials should be asked to report their version of events during the time they served. Brief transcripts or summaries, with tape counter numbers, should be made of the interviews quite soon after they are finished and copied. These serve as indexes to the subjects of the tapes, and can be scanned by the researcher to see if it is worthwhile to listen to the tape itself. A file of cards listing the tapes as they are acquired should also be kept as a catalog for the use of the public.

The master or original tape should be removed

Tape cassettes labelled on the front and spine, with a numbered tape summary.

from storage and rewound at least once a year to prevent formation of magnetic spots which cause erasure or distortion of the sound. The copy tapes should also be rewound if they have not been used. Some very important current events, such as speeches and celebrations, may be taped and included in the collection—but they should be very special occasions. Such tapes are not ordinarily considered oral history. For a more complete discussion, see Willa Baum's *Oral History for Local Historical Society* and *Transcribing and Editing Oral History*.

Ephemera

Much valuable local history material is embodied in the type of material called *ephemera*—materials which were produced to be used once and thrown away. Ephemera is used to classify such things as programs, menus, organizational reports, handbills, funeral and sales notices, wedding announcements, sales slips, advertisements and posters, ballots, report cards—any item used to pass information on from person to person, and particularly one that mentions names, places, dates. Many pamphlets fall into this class, but pamphlets can usually be handled best as monographs. Ephemera is often printed on very poor quality paper; it usually has been folded and exposed to dirt and weather, and often the year is not given if a date is mentioned. Any identification or dates should be pencilled lightly on the back after the item is cleaned and flattened. The items are then placed in envelopes or folders in a filing case, arranged by subject. Here they are protected, available, and since items can be continually added, extremely informative.

Clippings in the ephemera file.

Clippings

Clippings are an especially valuable type of ephemera. Articles can be clipped by a staff member or volunteer, or they can be given to the collection by someone who clipped them at home. As gifts they sometimes come singly, sometimes as an envelope full, sometimes pasted in a scrapbook. It is fortunate when they are loose or pasted into scrapbooks on a subject basis, because then they are easier to straighten, flatten, protect, and include in the ephemera file.

A clipping file from the local paper, constantly maintained, with each clipping identified on its margin by newspaper, date, and page, filed by subject, can serve as a good index to local history. It may be an indexing aid to the local newspaper. In collecting the clippings, make sure that the subject is germane to local history, that source, date, and subject are noted. See that the clippings are protected from wear and tear; they should be mounted and placed in folders or envelopes. If funds are available, encasing clippings in mylar or triacetate is recommended.

Good quality rag or acid-free paper is the best material for mounting. The clipping should be pasted onto the sheet with very thin flour paste, and pressed until dry. The edges of the mounting sheet should surround the clipping entirely, to take the wear and tear of storage and handling. If you use uniform mounting sheets, the 8-½" x 11" size of good bond, the pages will not crease or bend in storage. Plain manila folders can be used to hold the mounted clippings in document boxes or file cases. If more sturdy mounting is needed, Permalife paper is best, again used with flour paste. A recipe for flour paste is given in "mending" section.

Clippings should be backed with acid-free paper and enclosed in a protective envelope of either plastic or acid-free material.

One staff member should be responsible for the ephemera files. Volunteer help is especially desirable in collecting ephemera and clippings, but some one person must be responsible for placing the material in the file, for retrieving and collating it. Without constant care, the file will become either a jumble or a skeleton—stripped of items that flesh it out. The decisions about subject headings and filing should also be made by this person, because of his or her knowledge of relationships to other materials and to needs in the collection.

Manuscripts

The category of manuscript materials covers such items as memoirs, diaries, journals, reminiscences, school essays, club minutes, business records and collections, church records, collections of letters, school reports, unbound theses and dissertations, and memorabilia. Each item is usually the only one in existence, and is quite often hand-written, although the phrase covers typed, or even mimeographed materials. These materials are valuable parts of a local history collection, but they pose special problems in ownership, processing, and servicing. Sets of records, such as the secretary's papers, or president's papers of a church, school club, business, civic group, political party, or other community organization are valuable materials, and they require special handling and a great deal of room for storage. They must be kept together as a unit, in the order in which they originated. They are usually worth all the care they require, which includes cleaning, storage, and maintenance.

As they become available, such things as diaries and memoirs and collections of letters add greatly to the depth and value of the collection. They delineate the realities of local history, and make events and people seem much more alive than generalized history. These details are of such value that if they do not exist, or cannot be found, it may become necessary to secure them through an oral history program. There is no substitute for an eyewitness account, and often the diary, or journal, or letter home is the most colorful account that there is.

Correspondence, especially personal letters, is very important. There can either be bundles of letters tied together, or a box of letters from various writers, or a single letter saved because it described an event of interest or importance. Each letter must be opened, read, flattened, and protected. In a local history collection, the writer does not need to have been a person of importance; the letter can be of

Manuscript materials are often done on poor quality paper and arrive at the library in a bad state of preservation.

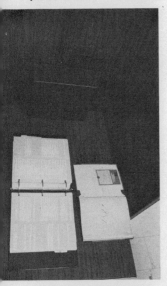

A diary from 1881 and an obituary listing of notable local people are interesting pieces of local history.

interest because it describes a time or place that is gone, or some happening so ordinary that other people seldom mentioned the subject.

Ownership and legal rights are important in the care and collection of personal papers that predominate in manuscript collections. When used for research and writing, they must be quoted exactly and cited with great care. Understanding the background that produced the papers is an important part of curatorship. Personal papers or manuscript collections take almost as much work and expertise in handling as photographs, and the rewards are almost as great. The papers themselves must be handled an item at a time, and a guide or index must be prepared ultimately to protect the papers from excessive handling. The papers must be stored together and in safe, acid-free folders and such boxes as Hollinger makes for the storage of manuscripts and documents, or in individual folios or portfolios.

Fortunately, the collection and care of manuscripts is described in depth in a new book, *Modern Manuscripts,* by Kenneth Duckett, available from the American Association for State and Local History. This book should be acquired when personal papers become an important part of a local history collection.

Memorabilia

Memorabilia takes many forms, but usually it is small souvenir objects. Printed material, such as menus, programs, or sales slips may be included in the ephemera collection. Do not hesitate to refuse items of memorabilia that more properly belong in a museum; refer the donor to the appropriate museum and transfer such items already acquired. Documentary collections deal with documentation and not with objects. If a clear definition of the items to be collected is not drawn up and adhered to, materials needed to build the documentary collections, such as diaries and newspapers and broadsides

Memorabilia can take many forms.

may be superseded in donors' minds by such items
as rock collections and wedding dresses from seven
different families. People tend to give what they feel
is appreciated, and there is a human tendency to
give showy, ego-building things to a library or museum. While the rock collection and wedding dresses
are of value in themselves, they would be better
placed in a minerals display or a house restoration
than a local history documentary collection.

A written policy statement about the goals,
methods, and materials needed in the local history
organization should also spell out the responsibility
taken for documents and objects; this will simplify
the tactful declining of artifacts with no documentary value. One or two souvenir items such as medals
can be accepted if they come in as part of a larger
collection; they can be handled as "illustrations" of
the accompanying documents. Usually there are ci-
tations with medals, and if they are in a larger collection they are handled as part of that miscellany.

Collections

Sometimes a local person gives a mass of materials
in many formats to the institution. If the subject of
the collection is homogeneous, it is usually wise to
keep the collection together, stored in a Hollinger
or other storage box, and cataloged or indexed as
the "Smith Collection" under the proper subject
heading or headings. If the collection covers more
than three subjects, this plan would not be feasible,
unless the donor were a person of such importance
that any interests of his would illuminate other areas
of history.

Sometimes the donor insists that the materials be
kept together. If they are about one or two subjects
the request is easy to grant, but the decision about
what to do with the material and how to do it must
rest with the curator or librarian. If the subject mat-
ter varies widely the collection would probably be
most useful distributed with the other subject mate-

*A collection of books on
regional history, donated by
a single family, is kept as a
unit. An index to such a
special collection is very
helpful to researchers and
staff.*

rials in the collection, with proper credit to the donor.

Gifts of materials in collections that do not deal with the local area should be declined. To be included in a local history collection the material must elucidate the life in the locale rather than the interests of a local donor.

Maps and Measured Drawings

Both area maps and small localized maps are of great importance in local history. Of special interest are the sketch maps which local people draw showing locations that never appear on larger commercial maps. These may be of farms, ditches, tram routes, buildings, and other geographic details that are subject to change of ownership or structure. Singular happenings in a spot may be recorded by a sketch map, and may be the only clue as to its exact location, because even such landmarks as rivers and buildings change. Some small maps appear in pamphlets or on sales handbills or advertising posters. Save blueprints to commercial structures or residences if they come your way. Artist's sketches of buildings, parks, farms, or houses and architect's plans contribute a great deal to knowledge of a local scene. Hand-drawn sketches are often done on poor quality paper. Plans of amateur builders can be crudely executed; most are probably work- and weather-worn. They are well worth saving, however, along with state, city, gasoline company, and travel maps.

Maps may be cumbersome to preserve and store, but they are valuable resources

With the rise of the historic preservation movement, historic areas and historic buildings are finally receiving needed attention and funds. Federal involvement in preservation received a boost in the 1930s with the establishment of the Historic American Building Survey (HABS); in 1971 the Historic American Engineering Record was set up. These agencies produce photographs, measured drawings, and reports on structures worthy of national attention: private and public buildings, homes, and now bridges and factories. The Library of Congress and your State Historic Preservation Office may have other architectural records. If they apply to your area, copies of the HABS and HAER records and those of other agencies would be a valuable addition to a local history collection.

Maps and drawings should be cleaned, straightened, flattened, and stored in map cases or on shelves. They can be rolled for storage just like textiles. If they are subject to much use, maps should be framed or mounted according to good museum practices. They may also be copied photographically to secure a use copy and to preserve the original.

A basic book collection, newspapers, photographs and some ephemera can give a local history collection a personalized identity that is available to a community in no other way. If there is an absolute lack of printed or written materials on the area, a taping program may be the only means of securing the facts and flavor of local history. The important points to record in local history, in print, in sound, or in picture, are people's names, place names, dates, and a sense of immediacy. These are the very stuff, the warp and woof, of history.

While the materials are being collected and analyzed and put together with items related to them in subject, if not in format, the curator will be finding strengths, weaknessess, gaps, and problems. The need for policies, and policy statements, and procedure guides is now apparent. These policies should be formulated and gathered into a looseleaf notebook as the process continues. They can be based on the facts given here, or located in other sources such as are listed in the Bibliography, or the result of consulting your state historical society. But they must be, and they can be, adapted to your own local history and local history collection as it grows.

4 Legal Aspects

Ownership

The ownership of documentary materials is, under ordinary circumstances, protected by the laws of purchase, by special legal ordinances such as those establishing libraries and museums, or by rules and regulations of an institution. Published materials are protected by copyright, which has been revised recently by Congress.

Local history materials are no exception to these general laws of copyright and ownership. Much that is unique and valuable in a collection—unpublished letters, manuscripts, photographs, memoirs, tape recordings—are protected by the state statutes, which usually provide that these personal, unpublished materials are the property of the writer or producer, and/or his heirs and assignees. They must not be used except with the permission of the owner or owners. Materials published from 1906 on are now protected by the new copyright law.

Deeds of Gift

Ownership of local history materials is assigned to a local history collection by a deed of gift from the producer, heir or heirs of the producer, or the assignee who legally gives up his interest. This deed of gift can be a simple form describing the material and giving it to the institution. Or the owner may loan the material for copying and give the rights to use and disbursal to the institution. When filled out, signed and dated, the deed will protect the institution in the use of the material, since it gives

37

City of Englewood

3400 South Elati Street
Englewood, Colorado 80110

Phone (303) 761-1140

(Date) _____

   The Englewood Public Library acknowledges the receipt of the
following items from

_____ (Name)

_____ (Address)

These items are:

☐ A gift to the Library

☐ On loan for _____ (Length of time)

☐ If on loan, may they be copied?   ☐ Yes   ☐ No

(Owner)_____

(Library)_____

rights to possession, use and protection of the material. A simple deed of gift is shown.

There are many more forms of this type: those authorizing the copying of borrowed materials, authorizing use of photos for one publication, and many other such detailed legalities. The Society of American Archivists has published a book of forms, called the *Forms Manual,* which may be studied for details. It is available from:

> The Society of American Archivists
> University of Illinois at Chicago Circle
> Box 8198
> Chicago, Illinois 60680

This manual contains forms from most states, and so is valuable for study. Before any forms are worked out by an institution, however, it is wise to consult your state historical society about *their* forms and any special details in deeding gifts that they have encountered. They will probably be happy to send sample deeds that conform to state law.

When material is accepted as a gift, it must be accompanied by a deed of gift, signed, and dated. A place on the deed allows for the recording of restrictions on the usage of the material, such as not making the material public for a stated length of time (perhaps a period of twenty-five years, or the lifetime of the donor's children). Without this opportunity to restrict public access to them, the gifts might not be given, especially if the material is sensitive. These restrictions are a means of protecting the privacy of individuals but at the same time providing for access to facts in the course of time. A carbon or a duplicate of the deed of gift, again signed by both parties to the transaction, may be kept by the donor of the gift as a receipt.

When a person uses material in a sensitive area in a local history collection, it is wise to keep a record of the user, the date, and the purpose of research. This is particularly important in the case of any items on which restrictions have been placed. These use records should be filed with the deeds of gift.

Appraisals

Gifts of local history materials, particulary if they are of the kind that could be sold to an antique or book dealer, are usually tax-deductible. This raises the question of evaluation and appraisal. The second deed of gift, or a regular receipt given the donor is *his* record for tax purposes. *The accepting institution does not make evaluations or appraisals.* They are the responsibility of the donor. In cases of gifts of considerable value, the donor hires a qualified appraiser and pays his fee, although the appraisal must be done in the accepting institution after the gift is accepted. Except for maintaining the gift for use and inspection if required, the accepting institution has no interest in the tax claims of the donor of the gift.

When asked to suggest an appraiser, the question can be referred to the state historical society, or the nearest National Archives and Records Center. Also consult AASLH publications *Modern Manuscripts* by Kenneth W. Duckett, and Technical Leaflet 97, "Appraisals."

Evaluation

The value of materials in a local history collection depends a great deal on their physical condition, and the amount of identification and authenticity they have—facts establishing who, what, when, where, why, and how. When a gift is accepted, it is wise to ask many questions about the material and to record the facts clearly, both on the deed of gift and on the material itself. All material should be identified as to source, or as the archivists say, to *provenance.* Archivists want to know in whose custody materials have been, as well as source. Conflicting details as to the provenance or custody of the material should be recorded and discrepancies in fact noted, because at some time the accuracy of the details may be determined, perhaps by persons using the materials. Someone of the collection staff, either paid or volunteer, should be responsible for research on the subject of the gifts. Identification of all gift material should begin as soon as possible after receipt and before processing. Often display and discussion of the gift within the institution stimulates interest, identification, information, and even further gifts.

Copyright

Newspaper and magazine articles, handbills, brochures, and other *published* items, intended for public information and dissemination, formerly were covered by the old copyright law. Unpublished works were covered by common law or state statute. The new copyright law replaces this dual system with a single federal statutory law which protects both works copyrighted after September 19, 1906, and all unpublished works as of January 1, 1978. Consult the U.S. government pamphlet for a full explanation of the schedule of copyright renewals between 1906 and 1978. Anything copyrighted before the 1906 date is considered "in the public domain"— the copyright protection has expired. These works are subject to the laws of libel, but usually problems in this area would have arisen upon publication. By the time they have arrived in a local history collection, these publications may be used, copied and quoted. Works still under copyright are subject to "fair use" restrictions which are defined under the new copyright law.

It is important that those responsible for the collection know which materials are copyrighted and what areas the new law covers.

5 Conservation

Local history materials are frequently old and fragile. They require special care to make them useable and to make them last. This is particularly true of materials produced since 1880, either written or printed, since most paper produced since then is of high acid or sulfide content. These papers yellow, tear or disintegrate very easily. Most of the materials we collect in local history appear on this kind of paper; for instance both old and new newspapers readily yellow and tear. If we use papers from early in this century too much, they come apart in our hands. Old photographs fade, get dirty, or lose corners and identification. Often the important manuscript is a set of memoirs written in a light pencil on a penny tablet. Gift materials come to us simply shoved into a box that has been in the corner of the barn for fifty years. These and other materials, such as tapes and microfilms, require special storage. All these circumstances mean that conservation of the unique materials of a local history collection, while sometimes bothersome, is tremendously important.

It is sufficient in most cases to straighten, flatten, brush clean, and safeguard materials by placing them in protective covers, thus keeping them from heat, light, and vermin. If the material is bulky, fragile, and liable to a great deal of use, as with files of newspapers, it is probably best to microfilm it for everyday use. Items that are not bulky, such as letters, important broadsides, or very fragile items, should be xeroxed or photographed so that the copy can be used and the original never disturbed. These decisions should be made during the cleaning and assessing steps.

Each item acquired must be individually handled
and assessed before it is incorporated into the collection. At this stage the curator examines the content of the material, decides if and where it fits into
the collection, and reviews the details of ownership
and the record of the gift and any restrictions. Cleaning the material proceeds at the same time.

Cleaning

If the local history materials come in bundles or
packets, the packets must be cleaned before they
are opened. Use a soft brush, such as a shaving brush,
a good quality paint brush, or a camel's hair art
brush. Then each item must have all surface dust
brushed off, as well as simple molds. Old pins or
paper clips, which are usually rusty, or old rubber
bands, which have disintegrated and stuck to the
paper, must be removed very carefully. Pages should
be straightened out, with folds and wrinkles removed. Sometimes the paper is too dry and brittle
to flatten satisfactorily, so after all surface dirt is
brushed off it must be humidified.

Items having no relationship to the collection or
to local history, duplicates, if there are several, and
such items as envelopes that have no address, date,
postmark, or stamp can be discarded. Clean un-
marked pieces of good quality paper, even little ones
used in letters to preserve privacy of the message
should be saved; they can be used by a trained
conservator for mending or restoring pages and
books.

Humidifying

In her early book about caring for paper, *The
Repair and Preservation of Records*, Adelaide
Minogue stated that in desperate cases, one could
humidify large sheets of paper by placing them in
a large commercial shortening can, standing the
sheets in a circle about the edges, and placing a cup

of water in the center. Left for 24 hours with the lid tightly on the can, the sheets would absorb enough moisture to become workable. The modern equivalent of the lard can is the large plastic garbage can with a tight fitting lid.

A sealed box of some kind is very useful in caring for paper, both in humidifying and in decontaminating the paper of mold or insect infestation. The easiest kind of a sealed box to acquire is a refrigerator with a broken cooling system, but which has good seals around the door, and a good quantity of racks. These are often available for anything from hauling away to not more than $25.00. Hydrometers are inexpensive, available in hardware stores, and useful for reading humidity in both the box and in storage areas of a local history collection.

Place the materials to be humidified on the racks of the box, a couple of saucers of water in the bottom of the box, and leave sealed for 12 to 24 hours, or until the hydrometer registers at least 30 percent humidity. The papers can then be flattened with no danger of cracking or tearing.

Decontaminating

If any evidence of blue or green mold or stains appear during the brushing, the paper should be decontaminated. People working with old papers should wear masks to protect themselves from these old molds, as well as old dust. Simple paper masks are available at most hardware stores or drug stores; even simple ones give protection. The molds can be killed in the same box used for humidifying.

Thymol crystals are easiest to use for killing mold and fungus. They are available from scientific supply houses, or from your local druggist. If he does not have them, he will be able to get them for you. A 40-watt light bulb that does not go off when the door is closed is also needed. The papers are placed on the racks of the box, and a saucer of thymol crystals is placed over the lighted bulb. As the heat from

Be sure there is adequate fire protection for your collections. Consult the local codes department or fire marshal.

the bulb rises, the crystals will begin to evaporate, creating an antiseptic-smelling vapor. In 48 hours in the sealed box, the thymol vapor will decontaminate the paper.

Insect infestation should be counteracted by use of moth crystals in the box for a few days and in the storage area later.

The effects of these treatments are safe for paper but unknown for photographs. Black and white prints can be treated with 1% aqueous solution of Hyamine 1622 and negatives with Kodak film cleaner.

Abrasives and Erasers

When brushing does not remove localized spots of soil from papers, another method of cleaning is needed. The use of erasers may occasionally be required, but these are abrasive cleaners and can, in the hands of an inexperienced worker, result in fraying and tearing paper. Absorene wallpaper cleaner, used carefully in a blotting manner, is the least harmful cleaner, but it does not remove any dirt with grease in it. Opaline dry cleaning bags are also used to "blot" dirt from paper. These are soft bags of rubber or soap eraser dust, and can be purchased at art supply stores. They are good for removing localized dirt. Art gum erasers are easier to come by, and are the standard, inexpensive way to remove localized dirt. They tend to be harder on paper than the above two erasers. Conservators occasionally resort to the standard pink pearl eraser; used by a professional, it does not harm paper. Only trained people should attempt cleaning beyond the preliminary brushing and removal of pins and rubber bands, however. Remember, nothing should be done to documents that is not completely safe and completely reversible.

If you have valuable papers that need more cleaning, such as removal of sticky scotch tape or scotch tape stains, save them for a trained conservator. One of the most hopeful things going on in the history, museum, and library fields at the present time is the establishment of regional conservation centers, where valuable items from the area can be cared for. Keep your attention on what is happening in this field in your area, and keep lines of communication open so that you can take advantage of such places if you need them. As your collection grows you will need them, because many aspects of caring for valuable documents must be left to a trained conservator.

Flattening

Papers are often found folded from storage in old-fashioned files, or from placement in envelopes, or simply from having been shoved someplace. After they are dusted and humidified, it is easy to flatten them either by pressing them between blotters in a binder's press or a letter press, or by smoothing them with a warm iron, again between blotters. For curled or wrinkled photos, use recommended photographic blotters for flattening.

When unfolding papers, be careful not to bend fragile paper backward from a fold. It is a very natural thing to do, but it can break a fold completely in two. Instead, humidify the paper, and carefully press the wrinkles out with a bone folder, and then iron or press.

Make absolutely sure that all dust and dirt, and especially residue from erasing, if you have used an eraser, is removed from the paper before you flatten it. When the papers are flattened they may be placed in protective containers, and stored flat.

One of the main topics of discussion among conservators and curators of papers is deacidification. It is of great importance in major collections, but it is no undertaking for persons without conservation laboratories. In a small collection, proper storage, microfilming and other methods of preserving a collection are much more practical.

After cleaning and flattening, materials should be placed in protective covers before they are placed in storage. Acid-free folders and covers are available from supply houses. Wrapping bundles of newspapers in brown paper protects them from light and dirt, and enables them to be moved more easily than when loose. Manila file folders and Hollinger boxes are the usual storage for flattened materials, if they are not stored flat in portfolios.

The goal of this conservation effort is to keep local history materials safe, clean, and together until better systems or more money for their care is available. For these reasons, take care in all cleaning and restoration work. Use safe materials always. Never use scotch tape. Good quality stainless steel paper clips, with a small piece of acid-free paper between the documents and the clip, may be used to keep papers together. Cleaning in appropriate ways, simple mending, and proper storage of materials will probably preserve local history materials for as long as they are needed. If they are being used frequently, copy the materials on microfilm or photograph them. None of these processes will harm the originals, they will keep the fragile materials from unnecessary use. In cleaning and mending unique materials, it is better to do nothing than to do the wrong thing.

Mending and Mounting

Mending and mounting of materials should always be done in the simplest manner possible, with the simplest tools. The things that damage paper and photos and all the materials of a local history collection are light, contaminated air, insects, mold, dirt, and wear and tear. Improper repair can be equally as damaging. The use of the wrong papers, pastes and glues, or tapes for mending can damage a book or paper beyond repair. For mounting papers, maps, or photos, use a good quality rag paper board. Acid-free board is readily available from art supply stores, or from library or archival supply houses; a good

Loose book spines can sometimes be repaired with a special glue, available from library suppliers.

brand is Permalife from Hollinger. Pure cotton organdy or muslin, washed to remove sizing, is good for mounting maps. They can then be rolled and slipped into plastic sleeves and stored on shelves with labels so that they do not have to be unrolled to be identified. Japanese tissue, available from the library supply houses, is needed for mending. All these are best used with a home-made flour paste. When mending or mounting, the paste should be used very thin, and spread with a small paint brush. Pasted items should be placed between two sheets of waxed paper, then between sheets of blotter and pressed, either in a book press (often called a binder's bond), an old letter press, or between boards with weights. Paper for mending tears, or Japanese tissue, should always be torn and not cut, because the fibers bond much better when torn. If a ragged tear is being mended, be sure that the edges are carefully aligned. The mend should be pressed between blotters, and the blotters changed every few minutes for the first half hour to prevent cockling of the mend.

Large items, such as handbills that are coming to pieces, should be mounted on a sheet of Japanese tissue or acid-free board. Small prints or letters may sometimes be hinged into a folder with a cover that is cut out to allow the print to be studied without being handled. Make hinges of Japanese tissue, and use the ordinary flour paste. The paste may be made or secured dry from a library house such as TALAS. Folders should be made of acid-free material.

The requisites for a basic cleaning and mending program in a local history collection are a table to work on, a letter press or binder's bond, good mending materials, a few simple tools, and a great deal of patience. Local history materials cannot be hurried.

The paste recipe:
1 cup of wheat flour, beaten with enough cold water to make cake batter consistency. Put into batter ¾ or ⅞ pint boiling water, and beat smooth. Put over flame, stirring constantly and scraping the sides of the pan. Cook 5 minutes after it begins to boil and thicken. Add 1 tablespoon formaldehyde when cool, and store in covered jar. Add water to thin before use.

Storage

When the materials are cleaned, protected by a casing of some kind if needed, and ready to be put away, they can be placed on the shelves of a locked case, or placed by subject in the local history case or file. You may want them placed in storage areas away from public access. Items should not be stored without protection: a slip case, a periodical binder, an acid-free folder, or a brown paper wrapping. Large groups of documents are best stored in folders in document boxes on shelves. All of these will protect the materials from dust, light, excess handling, and wear and tear.

Filing cases are often used for storing local history materials. They are not really good storage for the materials, because the materials cannot be laid flat. If the cases are filled enough to give the sheets support, the materials will be harder to extract. This means that the documents get crumpled and torn, or they slip down, get rounded, and get crushed. Document boxes on shelves are more satisfactory because they can be filled with folders for support, and permit easier retrieval of materials. Generally speaking, money is better spent for steel shelving and document boxes that for steel filing cabinets.

In ideal conditions materials are protected from light, particularly fluorescent lights, and are stored at temperatures of 60° to 70° F. and a humidity of 30 to 40 percent. Since this environment is ideal for people, there should be no problem in judging if the documents are safe. They are, if their custodians are comfortable, albeit a little cool. We should all like to have air-conditioning and humidity control, but if these are not available, use the old devices: pull the blinds in summer, put pans of water on the heaters in winter. If people can survive, so can the materials.

It is much better for the materials to be cared for, and about, in a local history collection than to be left in a hot dusty attic, or cold, damp cellar. Never give up collecting local history materials just because conditions are not ideal. Just do the best thing possible under present conditions; more local history has been saved on the shelves of a small historical so-

Storage space is always a problem. Do not hesitate to refuse gifts that do not add to the better understanding of your area.

Indiscriminate collecting can lead to the sandwiching of valuable items with those of marginal worth. Be selective.

ciety or library and in brown paper wrappings than by any amount of air-conditioning.

Labelling

Never store or shelve anything without labelling it. Write on the back or margin of single items in no. 2 pencil. Write on wrapped packages with a felt-tipped pen. Place labels inside the sleeve of wrapped maps and photos so that they can be read through the sleeve if it is plastic, or pasted on the outside if it is not. Always have the labels clear, detailed, and conspicuous enough that you know what is in the package without opening it. If material is stored in boxes, either temporarily or permanently, the box should be clearly labelled as to content and source. When an item is removed from a box for use, this should be clearly indicated on the box so that the item is returned to the proper place in the proper box. Box labels can be run off on inexpensive paper with a mimeo machine and pasted on the boxes. The form for duplication should be devised with enough space for a description of the contents and for its use history. The record should show both removal and return of the item, and who used it.

Document boxes, preferably acid-free, and metal shelving are best for all kinds of materials storage.

One thing becomes very obvious in working with local history materials: no one ever complains about too much identification or too much labelling, but much work and worry has resulted from carelessness about it or lack of it.

Microfilming

By far the easiest way to acquire, preserve, use, and store bulky items such as newspapers is with microfilm. Most state historical societies have extensive collections of local newspapers on film and sell positive prints for a reasonable charge. They also have lists of local newspapers on microfilm; if you need a list of papers that once existed in your state or area, they can help you find it. If you should locate a file of local newspapers, (perhaps in the owner's family or publisher's office) that the state society does not have on film, they may microfilm it and make a positive copy for the discovering institution, again at a reasonable cost. They will retain the negative, and a research positive for their collection. The original file is usually returned to the owner, although often they do make a gift of it to one institution or the other. The new find should also be listed in all the newspaper finding aids. This process guarantees the availability of the newspaper and provides a great service to the historical researcher both nationally and locally.

If a society library wishes to have papers or other materials microfilmed, it should try first to set up an arrangement with the state historical society. If the state society cannot help, get a local firm in the state or area interested in the project to do the job. It is very costly to set up an in-house microfilming system. A local firm will work diligently to meet the specialized needs of the collection, and to assist preserving local history. It is well to bear in mind that such firms as banks have microfilming equipment to keep track of banking records, and they could assist. This might give less professional results than a firm that specializes in microfilming, but it may be best for both the borrower and lender to keep it local. Since standards are set for microfilming, an adequate job can be assured. See the material published by the Library of Congress or National Microfilm Association in the Bibliography. Much of the preliminary work, such as the laborious collating of the papers to repair tears and the notation of missing issues or pages, could be done by volunteers. Thus labor costs would be reduced and warnings of missing material would be included in the film.

Microfilm readers, essential to the use of the film after you have secured it, are becoming more compact and relatively inexpensive. When considering the purchase of a reader, consult new catalogs and information through a local audiovisual dealer or

Microfilm readers and reader-printers are now more compact and easier to thread.

by writing to your state historical society. Since reader models change often, it is not wise to use old catalogs or information. A local dealer will be of assistance in servicing a machine as well as installing it. If you know nothing about readers or microfilm publications, a good way to learn would be to attend the exhibits of your state library association convention. Such firms as University Microfilm usually have booths and display their equipment. They also have catalogs of such things as university theses and dissertations on film; it is amazing the nuggets of local history that show up in undergraduate and graduate theses. Check local universities and colleges for theses as well as the film catalog.

Collations and Restricting Use

One of the most important means of preserving local history materials is by restricting access. Keep materials in closed and locked cases and supervise their use carefully. When a user is returning materials, they should be collated. This is the old library technique of checking the material, in the presence of the user, to make sure that all parts are present, in order, and in proper condition. With such diverse materials in a local history collection as photos, clippings, and maps, each item should at least be counted when it is taken from the file, and counted again upon return.

The use of a check-out card—a colored sheet or card to identify spots from which material was removed for use, and listing the user's name—is very helpful both in collation and reshelving material. Preprinted check-out cards are usually available from stationers or library and business supply houses. It would be much less expensive to mimeograph your own on colored paper, however.

Time spent supervising the use of local history materials and in collating is well spent, because your materials are unique, and if they are lost or misplaced they are usually gone forever.

6 Processing

Processing is the procedure by which documentary materials are prepared for inclusion in a collection. It is the step between acquisition, with its fiscal and legal responsibilities, and the servicing of the materials for the public. It is the means by which the materials are accounted for both as they are acquired and as they are used, and it is the key to finding the item that is wanted from among the masses of the material.

In libraries this part of the procedure is called "technical processes." In archives it is called "arrangement and description." In either process, or where local materials are handled by a combination of the two methods, the desired result is intellectual control of the material for use, and maximum protection of the material in storage.

Cataloging

Regular library cataloging is not satisfactory for local history materials except for items which can be handled as monographs. The problem of handling materials that come in as single ephemeral items or as a collection often precludes the use of monograph cataloging. Materials must nonetheless be accessioned, inventoried, and listed so that they are recorded and available for use, as in the book catalog and shelf list. They must also be shown in relationship to other materials, as in the subject catalog. Provision must also be made for constant addition of materials.

These controls are managed by using finding aids that list materials as items or groups of items accord-

A local history collection, cataloged by subject.

ing to subject. Access is by subject heading or by index. Since most local historians seem to want information in depth and detail rather than from an encyclopedia approach, they usually prefer to have a great deal of material to study. They also want to use all such materials as tapes, photos, newspapers or other materials that illuminate their chosen subject.

For this reason the list of subject headings for photos, for ephemera, for monographs must all be the same. The headings must grow out of the materials available in the collection, and must be unique to and illustrative of the locale and the collection. Photos or ephemera should be collected in some quantity and studied before subject headings are decided upon. Headings are expandable, of course, as materials are added to the collection, or as new subjects become important in local history. Once the headings are established, however, they can be the key to an entire local history collection.

The subject headings of a local collection could be:

ENGLEWOOD   GENERAL HISTORY

Englewood   Before 1900
               1900–1909
               1910–1919
               1920–1929
               1930–1939
               1940–1949
               1950–1959
               1960–1969
               1970–1979
               1980–

Bridges   Maps
Buildings   Minorities
Businesses   Negroes
  Alexander Aircraft   Natural Features (NF)
  Alexander Film Co.   Organizations
Churches   Parks
City Hall   Police
Elections   Recreation
Fire Department   Residences
  (Volunteer Fire Department) Schools
Floods 1917, 1927, 1933, 1965 Streets
                               Theatres

Government and Government Officials
Grocers
Holidays
Hospitals and Health
Industry
Library

Transportation
    Cherrelyn Horse Car
Water

Places

Castlewood	Littleton
Cherrelyn	Melvin
Cinderella City	Orchard Place
Clark Colony	Petersburg
Fiske's Gardens	Sheridan
Fort Logan	Sullivan
Ken Caryl	Tuileries

People—general, alphabetically

Cassidy	Jones
Chater	Kehoe
Dobbins	Staats
Dunn	Skerritt
Flood	Steck
Hardcastle-Erickson	Wollenweber.

These headings grew out of the materials in the collection. Almost any collection will use some of them—the general history and the breakdown by decades, the places and place names, the names of people, schools and churches. All these are the skeleton of local history anywhere. The unique items are what flesh out local history: the history of floods, of specialized transportation, the special importance of the volunteer fire department, and so on.

In ranching country, ranches and cattle would be main subjects; in mining country, mines, mills and miners. These subject headings have to grow from the available material and the area, and should be checked often against the book subject catalog and the materials themselves before they are finally established.

Once headings are established they can easily be expanded as materials are acquired. For instance, if a great many photos of the volunteer fire department come in, they can be distributed into decades in the history of the department. When there is not much on schools, all photos or all memorabilia (report cards, programs, annuals, etc.) can be grouped together. When the collection grows these items can be divided by the individual schools. This is the advantage of the system: any number of items can be added at any time, each where it will be most useful in relation to other materials in the collection.

Indexing

The ephemera and photographic files of a local history collection should be self-indexing. When consulted by subject all materials or references to them should be present for study. In some cases a "see" reference must be indicated if materials have been grouped under one subject heading rather than another.

If more information is available under other headings the "see also" reference should be used. It is also used for materials containing general and background rather than specific information. "See" (X) and "see also" (XX) references should be written directly on the file folders so that the patron can go from one to the other with no loss of thought.

Reference File

A library worker prepares a bibliography of a local history collection.

Indexing is needed for quick reference and to enable a quick overview of the material in the collection. A local reference file that serves as an index to the whole collection can be developed over a long period of time. As the collection grows and as people work with it, pieces of information will show relationships. As the collection is processed a card file should be established, on either 3″ x 5″ or 4″ x 6″ cards, containing references by subjects. Established headings are used for the entire collection. Photos, ephemera, clippings, newspaper references, book references may all be noted on these cards. This type of file is particularly needed for use with newspapers on microfilm. When a subject has been looked up

on the film, the card can be made and the same
subject found again in much less time than by going
through the roll of film. Many local history items are
worthy of inclusion, such as paragraphs in standard
state or county histories, or narratives from tape
recordings. The information does not have to be
copied, just the location of the information is enough.
Small items that have been clipped from magazines
or newspapers can be pasted right onto the card,
but in this case the name, date, and page number
of the source of the clipping must be typed on the
card also. Occasionally the clippings get torn or lost,
and the reference must still be useable. The clipping
itself should have the subject heading written on
it, and the card should be stamped with the name
of the collection, in case the clipping does come
loose.

Sample Reference Cards

PEOPLE

Charlesworth, Henry Dowd
Aug. 6, 1889—Oct. 15, 1956

Englewood council, 1919–1927
Mayor,   1936–1944

ENTERPRISE, Oct. 20, 1956 p.8
Ap. 20, 1936 p.1
Ap. 22, 1944
June 9, 1924

Englewood. STREETS

Renaming of streets, 1889

Englewood HERALD
Ap. 23, 1909, p.4

map, city boundary changes,
list of streets, 1889
list of streets, 1909

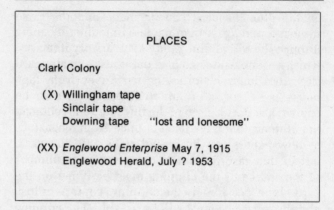

Storage

When materials in a local history collection must
be kept in a public area, legal-size filing cabinets
or lateral files with locks are probably the most
secure storage. If they can be kept in limited access
areas, the use of open shelves and acid-free document or storage boxes is better for the materials.
Monographs and periodicals are shelved as in a
library, preferably in locked cases. Photographs are
usually kept in separate files, with their own dividers
and headings, placed in groups in acid-free folders
or envelopes.

The ephemera, memorabilia, and other items are
kept in a general file, stored the same way, and all
serviced as a unit. Items are individually identified
as to subject heading and folder number in soft
pencil on a margin so that they can be returned to
the proper place, the folder with the same heading
and number. Ten items is a good number to assign
to each folder. It does not make the folder too bulky,
and it does not damage the material. It is also easy
to collate if there is a known number of items in
each folder. When there are ten items in the folder
a second one should be started, marked *Englewood
Streets #2* and filed right behind *Englewood Streets*.
Or, the streets on which material is available should
be subdivided: *Streets-Broadway; Streets-Fox.* By

keeping a predetermined number of photos or items of ephemera in envelopes, and seeing that they are returned there, an inventory and count of the local history materials is easily made. It is surprising how often librarians or curators are asked how many photos or other items are in a historical collection.

7 Services

Patrons seeking information in local history collections want to know general history, want the answer to a specific reference question, or want detailed material to use in some project. The first questions can usually be answered by producing a standard or general history book, or manuscript histories of the area. The second can be answered by using a reference file or reference books or directories. Persons working on the last type of question want to see everything possible that can give or suggest information or leads to information. They want to study and compare photos, sketches, maps, check photos against newspaper articles, and listen to tapes discussing the subject or even the period.

For these reasons all local history materials in a collection are entered under the one subject heading list and index headings. Then the patron can be shown index cards to newspaper files, all photo and ephemera folders, and all the references on the cards to the books or periodicals in the collection. Summaries or transcripts of tapes should have subject headings noted in them when the subjects are discussed, either in capital or red letters in the body of the summary or transcript, as well as being listed on the box. When all processed materials have been used and all the headings have been pursued, the librarian or curator can feel that the patron has seen everything available.

Retrieval

When a collection has been thoughtfully collected and carefully processed, the problems associated

with retrieval of the materials for use usually lie
in misplacing or losing items. Proper labelling and
collation can control these problems by keeping
materials together and intact. Careful shelving is also
important.

Pilfering of materials is a common problem, and
must be guarded against by allowing proper copying
facilities, and by collation. Newspapers or books are
often mutilated when the originals are used. Microfilming the documents precludes this type of de-
struction; so does immediate shelving and close
watch on materials being used. Most large research
libraries or archives restrict the number of items a
researcher can use at one time, which makes supervision a little easier. It is a good practice for small
institutions too.

Forms should be developed to control materials
and orders going out of the room or the building
for copying. They should be numbered sequentially
as they are used, and should contain the patron's
name, address, charges for material ordered, and
details of the order. One copy should be made for
the record, one for the photographer, and one for
the patron. These may be typed and mimeographed,
and all three may be color-coded by use—one color
for the society, one for the photographer or photo-
copier, and a different one for the patron. A sample
of this work order is included.

Usage

Rules for local history materials should be clearly
formulated in the policy and procedure book and
posted in the area in which they are used, or each
user should be handed a mimeographed sheet listing
them. These rules should state where materials can
be used, copying rules and rates, and the use of credit
lines. A sample is:

1. All local history materials are kept locked in
cases and must be requested at the desk.

WORK ORDER

_____

Date_____

Name_____

Address_____

Phone_____

KIND OF WORK:

	Number	Negative # or Subject

Photographic Prints _____

Slides_____

Microfilm _____

   Print-out_____

   Reels Positive_____   Negative_____

Copy Tape _____

Photocopy of Xerox _____

PROCESSING INSTRUCTIONS

   Size_____ Finish_____

_____

_____

_____

_____

PRICES Prints: 4 x 5 $2.50
                 5 x 7   3.50   Service charge for making negative
                 8 x 10 5.00 $1.50

      Photocopy, 15¢ per page
      Microfilm print-out, $1.50 per page
      Positive microfilm, $15.00 per reel

Materials will be used only by person making purchase, and all responsibility for this use is assumed by the purchaser. Materials should be credited to "Englewood Collection. Englewood Public Library".

Signature_____

Paid: date_____   Date promised _____

Amount:_____   Date finished_____

Delivered_____

2. All local history materials except certain clearly marked books must be used in the area, and should be collated upon return to the desk.

3. Printed materials may be copied if copyright provisions allow and if it can be done without damage to the materials, for 15¢ a page.[1]

4. Photographic copying of positive prints is done by the library upon written order from the patron. Charges are:

$$4'' \times 5'' \text{ print} \quad \$2.50$$
$$5'' \times 7'' \text{ print} \quad 3.50$$
$$8'' \times 10'' \text{ print} \quad 5.00$$

and must be paid for when ordered.

5. Only ball point pens or pencils may be used in doing research in local history materials; no fountain pens, or ink bottles. Never mark materials, even with a pencil.[2]

6. Any use of pictures or other materials should be credited as to source if printed or in speech. The form to use is "Englewood Collection, Englewood Public Library"; or "Jefferson County Historical Society, Local History Collection".[3]

Reporting to Other Agencies

When a reasonably informative collection has been assembled on an area, it should be made known. The local newspaper will be delighted to keep the immediate area informed, and nearby libraries will become aware of it. It should also be reported to researchers farther away. The first place to report holdings is your state historical society.

1. This price will naturally be the price charged for copying, but in an historical collection it is not wise to send a patron to a machine into which coins are fed. It is better that a staff member or volunteer handle the unique and fragile materials to prevent damage. Maybe the price will have to go up; in some research institutions the price runs up to $1.00 a page.

2. This is purely a research rule, and not be be confused with the rules for marking photos and ephemera.

3. This rule is not only to build the image of the institution or collection, it makes it much easier for later researchers when they know where things come from.

If newspapers are included in your collection they will probably make the report of your holdings to the national listings.
Report holding also to:

> *American Library Directory*
> R. R. Bowker Company
> 1180 Avenue of the Americas
> New York, N.Y. 10036.

If a good photo collection exists, it should be reported to:

> *Picture Sources*
> Picture Division, Special Libraries Association
> 235 Park Avenue South
> New York, N.Y. 10003

Large manuscript or research collections should be reported to:

> NUCMC
> National Union Catalog of Manuscript
> Collections
> Library of Congress
> Washington, D.C. 20540

The closest libraries and historical museums will be interested in your project, collections, and patrons. Nondocumentary materials that are outside the area of your holdings should be transferred to these collections. Their personnel will use your collections, and they will send you patrons. Good interrelationships among library, museum, and other local educational institutions will enrich everyone. At the same time library, museum, and local history materials will be in the proper collection, properly cared for, and used.

8 Training of Volunteers

The service given to persons asking questions about the local area, whether current or historical, has a great deal to do with establishing the value of a historical institution or collection to its community. Regardless of how good a collection is, if the service given to it is not complete, accurate, quickly and easily available, the institution is not performing its function. For this reason, in-service training in managing and servicing a local history collection must be developed. It should aim at training a staff that is fully committed to giving good service, and that understands the local area thoroughly. The training must aim at bringing the staff an awareness of policies, procedures, processes, and personnel in the area, the institution, and the collection. This goal requires training for new programs, and continuing training for regular and new personnel. Staff responsibilities must be assigned and delineated to prevent ragged service and gaps in the collection.

Local historical organizations or local historical collections in a public library are usually underfunded and must do without a large paid staff or enough professional assistance in starting or servicing their collections. Quite often organizations are made up of groups of persons who feel that the history is the essential thing; they volunteer to save it and face making a collection out of it when and as they can. The volunteer is the backbone of these organizations, whether all-volunteer or professionally staffed.

The director or librarian in charge of the collection should recruit volunteers actively or assign the task

to someone who understands the need for enthusiastic helpers. Volunteers must be trained, assigned,
and supervised to be effective. Whether volunteers
show up as individuals with an interest, or come
as a group determined to do their share of a job
they consider important, they must be trained just
as thoroughly as paid staff, and preferably at the
same time, so that the two groups can work as a
team. The head of the volunteers or the educational
director should hold regular classes in the geography,
history, and sociology of the locale, and provide
orientation into institutional policies and procedures—making sure new staff or volunteers can attend. Then assignments can be made and tasks accomplished with an understanding of the desired
outcome, and without too much detailed supervision.

Usually persons who volunteer to work in a historical collection do so because they have a need
for a constructive activity, an unusual interest in the
activity, or they have expertise to contribute. They
do not function well or productively if they are given
only routine chores or busy work, no training, and
no supervision and recognition. Undirected volunteers waste not only their own time and energy, but
also staff time and energy.

Areas of work in which volunteers function particularly well if trained and supervised are:

> clipping newspapers and filing clippings
> processing photographs or slides
> indexing for the reference file
> conducting a speaker's bureau
> oral history programs
> collecting and processing community
>   documents.

The first orientation classes for both staff and
volunteer should include discussion of the functions,
structure, and basic operating rules of the institution.
Then the volunteers must be thoroughly introduced
to the general and basic collections and materials
in the history of the area. They must read the books
that will make them knowledgeable about the area.

They must explore the geography and the background of the area and the community. Then they should study the materials in the collection to learn which of them illustrate the special history of the area. This reading of a basic book list, and studying the collection need not be done on supervised time. The reading list and shelf of books should be available for staff, volunteers, and patrons, and should consist of the basic book and periodical collection that make up the specialized collection. Usually there is a state history, or a regional history that is used in the schools and colleges in the area as a text. Several copies should be available; they are usually in paperback format, and fairly inexpensive.

When a volunteer has established a thorough background knowledge of both the area and the institution, he or she can express an interest in some special part of the work. Then specific assignments can be made. More work is accomplished if a volunteer is given an assignment and allowed to finish it than to assist with someone else's job. Each person so assigned should have available a copy of the policies and procedures of the institution as they relate to the specific task they have undertaken. This can be copied from the policy and procedure book. Further detailed instructions can be devised and briefly reproduced so that new staff members or volunteers will be able to do each operation according to policy and procedure, following instructions exactly and eliminating variations. Written instructions are essential for training, good habits, and producing uniformity in the collection. Instructions should be studied and discussed before beginning a project, consulted during the project, and checked upon completion. A sample of this type of instruction sheet for working with photos follows.

Instructions for Working with Photos

Work with photos should be done on a fairly large, smooth surfaced table without any other materials on it, so that items can be spread out and compared without getting any other materi-

als mixed up with them. The table should be clean, or covered with hard finished clean paper.

Materials

negatives, prints, original prints, slides.

ball point india ink pen for marking negatives.

ball point pen for marking slides.

#2 pencil for marking backs of prints. *Never use typewriter, ball point, or hard pencil for marking prints. They break the finish.*

negative envelopes or sleeves

slide containers

property stamp and stamp pad

photo files

photo forms if orders being processed.

RULES

1. Subject headings are assigned to new photos only by the curator of the collection.

2. Original writing on original prints, either front or back, is not erased. It is copied only onto the back of a copy print. If it is erroneous, a note of the error is made, with correction and source:

> "Bea Cook Collins says this Petersburg School was not in use in 1896, but that classes were held in the later two-story brick building. This earlier building was being used as a church. 4-27-73."

Donor and date of acquisition of photo are recorded.

PROCEDURES

1. Sort copy prints, originals, negatives, and slides, if any, into sets. If there is no negative, the original is ready to be laid aside for filing—after the subject heading is assigned and identification is completed.

2. Assign sequential negative number from master file to all items in the first set. Number negative. Write number in lower left corner on the back of original print and copy print.

3. Assign slide number to slide, if any. Write number on slide, and record on slide list. Record slide number in center of bottom of original and print.

Volunteers do their best when assigned to a project with some responsibility.

4. Write subject heading and explanatory material in complete and exact detail from original onto *copy* print, subject heading onto slide.

5. Write negative number, slide number, subject heading with all explanatory material onto negative envelope, with typewriter if possible.

6. Stamp copy print and slide with property stamp, lower right hand corner of print, bottom of slide.

7. Examine each part of set for completeness and correctness.

8. Sort negatives and prints into piles for filing. File prints by subject heading, slides and negatives by number.

9. Make sure that all materials are properly stored away, and that slide and negative numbers are properly posted on the master file for the next work session. Give all unclassified originals to the curator for heading.

10. Replace all forms in proper files, with orders to be picked up. Initial all forms for each process completed.

The curator of the collection will be responsible for assigning the subject headings, deciding which materials are to have prints and/or slides made, and for assigning the master negative number and slide number list. Please call attention of the curator to diminishing supplies.

It is especially important that a copy of instructions such as this be at hand at all times when new staff members or volunteers are working with a collection. It prevents error, and insures uniformity. A policy and procedure book, a senior staff member, or guide such as this book should always be available for consultation. Copies of reference rules and usage rules should be clearly posted in the local history area, and copies of these instructions and the policy and procedure book should be filed in the cases with the materials. Consultation takes time, but not as much as straightening out mistakes in procedure or judgment.

Volunteers must be given training, assignments, schedules, and supervision. Staff cannot relinquish authority or responsibility of a program to volunteers, but often the volunteer, when trained, can manage the first steps of a program, such as clipping newspapers, without ever leaving home.

9 Special Projects

Oral History

Oral history—as exemplified in folk tales, Bible stories, Homeric poems, and legends—is much older than written history. Future historians have a use and need for local history told and recorded by persons who have seen it happen. Fortunately for local history collections, the production of oral history, especially its technical features, has been greatly simplified. "How to" books have multiplied and special aids are becoming more numerous and accessible.

The basic tools of oral history are a tape recorder and a tape. The basic personnel are an interviewer and a story-teller or interviewee. The only other essential ingredient is a knowledge of the locale on the part of both parties, and some interviewing know-how on the part of the interviewer. The finished tape must contribute something to understanding the past of the area, observations on the present, or hope for the future to be included in a local history collection.

Before a taping program is even contemplated for a collection, a real assessment of the need for the program and the costs of the effort must be made. The costs must be figured in both time and money. It usually takes four to ten hours for a trained interviewer to make one hour of tape with a typed summary, and five to fifteen hours to a tape and transcript. This time must be taken into consideration, along with the costs of buying tapes and recorders. Care of the tapes after acquisition must also be considered, because tapes do take special storage and

70

scheduled rewinding and care. Their use also requires tape players for listeners.

Tape recorders are becoming simpler and quite inexpensive. Adequate models using cassettes are available in drug and discount stores as well as "sound" stores. The portable cassette recorder works on either house current or batteries. It is almost impossible to get cassettes into the machine wrong, unlike the older reel machines. The cassette recorder is also much easier to carry than the larger reel machine, and they do not seem to strike an inexperienced interviewee dumb as the large machines and reels did.

It is wise to consult a local dealer when planning an oral history program about tape recorders and tapes, transcribing and copying facilities. It is also wise to check with the school system, because they have often purchased some of this equipment to use in the foreign language classes. If the schools have such equipment as copying and transcribing equipment, it may be possible to borrow them, particularly during school vacation periods. In this case, equipment must be compatible. Locally bought equipment carries a certain kind of insurance: the dealer will be interested in the project and its success, and will probably be happy to contribute time and expertise to training the interviewer and seeing that the equipment is always in the best possible working order. He will also see that the best quality tapes for this kind of project are in stock and available, and will help the people in the project keep abreast of developments in a rapidly changing field.

An oral history program has the potential of adding unique sources of information to the history of an area.

Selection of the interviewer is tremendously important to the project. A great deal of background knowledge of both the community and the local history collection is necessary to produce recordings that contribute to the depth and breadth of the collection. The interviewer must have a thorough grasp of the questions that need answers, so that the interview adds to the total understanding of the area. A study must be made of areas in which history is lacking, and persons who can illuminate the areas must be selected as interviewees. A list of potential interviewees should be developed during preliminary research in the collection, in conjunction with the list of gaps to be filled; the list should be added to during the project from leads developed by other interviews or research.

A volunteer, or a team of volunteers, may be trained and assigned to the taping program, but the administration of the program should always be left in the hands of the curator of the collection. He or she can make note of the gaps as the collection develops. Filling these gaps should be the prime reason of a local oral history program.

Oral history tapes, like memoirs, diaries, and letters, are protected under the laws of ownership rather than by copyright laws. When a tape is to be made, a deed of gift or a release form must be filled out listing interviewer, institution, interviewee, restrictions, if any, and any books or documents used in providing sustantiation, documentation, or background. The deed of gift form used for other gifts to the institution will suffice. An introductory statement by the interviewer should also be recorded on each tape stating the name of the interviewer, the institution for which the tape is being made, the interviewee, the date, the place, and any unusual circumstances. This information should also be recorded on the tape label.

Some persons being interviewed find the use of photographs or documents very helpful in recalling the facts of local history. If these are used, and particularly if they are part of the local history collection, they should be clearly identified as part of the interview. If they belong to the interviewee, make an effort to secure them, or at least to copy them, for the collection. An oral history project tends to bring in quantities of documentary and illustrative material to a local history collection. Photos and oral history in particular are strongly interrelated.

Much has been written in the last few years about

the techniques of making tapes, the values of making oral history recordings, and caring for the tapes in storage. The Oral History Association was formed to report on and promote developments in the field; it publishes good bibliographies of the written materials. The American Association for State and Local History has also published helpful books and technical leaflets on oral history. Oral history is a specialized approach to local history, and a very good resource in building a collection, but it should be approached soberly, discreetly, and after much study of the literature of oral history. As a special project it can be a valuable addition to a local history collection.

Exhibitions

Putting local history materials on display can make many friends for a collection. Exhibits of materials in the collection tend to attract gifts, and often prove helpful in identification of persons or places. Exhibits of photographs and copies of newspaper articles make very interesting conversation-starters at annual meetings and open houses in an institution; they draw attention to the purposes of the organization and stimulate interest in its progress. The exhibit thus furthers the work of the institution.

Materials to be used in an exhibit must be selected with care. A few interesting items well displayed are much more effective than an unrelated, unconsidered group of photos or documents. Materials for exhibition must also be so prepared that the reasons for showing them are evident, but at the same time protecting them from light, dust, pollution, and the other enemies of local history materials.

A special exhibit of genealogy material in a local history section of a library.

Effective exhibits can be mounted by using mechanical copies of documents or good prints of photos rather than originals. Display and exhibition of the materials in a local history collection is as much a part of the business of a local history as is research. The curator has the same responsibility to preserve and protect the materials during exhibition as during research and reference uses.

Very clear directions for preparing documents for display and creating exhibition space can be found in the books and technical leaflets of the American Association for State and Local History and other museum associations. The uses of plexiglas, low lighting, Kodagraph to protect against ultra-violet light, and preparation of mylar, cellulose acetate, acid-free mounting board, and other protections for the materials are clearly explained. These techniques are within the capabilities of the staff or volunteers of even the smallest institution.

Community Records

Today there is a great need for the information contained in local government documents as a part of everyday living as well as part of the historical scene. The actions of local governments touch our everyday lives in many ways, yet communities do not always have a communication system that allows free access to this information. Any institution that could collect and make available the papers produced in the course of agency business would be performing a great public service. Libraries for many years have endeavored to collect state and federal documents, but local ones, if collected at all, were either cataloged as monographs, or dropped into the vertical files, where they were subjected to special stresses—use, loss, or misplacement. The publications of local government units are proliferating at the same rate as federal and state documents. They are becoming so numerous, and so important to our daily lives, that a real community service could be performed by systematically collecting, processing, and servicing them. If a local historical agency has the space, time, and staff, either volunteer or regular, it would add to the usefulness, prestige, and stature of the institution. By including these materials the local history collection would be enriched, and would gradually take on the characteristics of an archive.

If local government publications are collected,
they should, at least in the beginning, be handled
separately from other additions to the collection.
In a records program, everything in a series must
be collected as it is produced by an agency, but only
five or ten percent is worth keeping for a final collection or archive. The rest is discarded as its usefulness is over or a final disposition of the subject is
reached. The records keep track of the constantly
changing patterns, problems, growth, and structure
of local government, and thus reflect a locale. They
deal with statistics, officials, financial reports, and
governmental bodies and their activities. They are
often not as interesting or exciting as the usual materials of local history, but in the long run they tend
to be more important.

The key to arranging local government publications is to use as "author" the agency or unit that
produced them. The first step is obtaining an organizational chart of the governmental unit. It must be
detailed enough to outline the departments, bureaus,
commissions, boards, subdepartments and offices in
the city and county, and show how they interrelate.
The telephone directory, city reports, annual budgets, court house or city hall directories can all be
used to determine organizational structure if a chart
is not available. However, a chart which is developed
by this method should be taken to the city manager
or the county clerk to be checked for accuracy.

Looking in the phone book of an ordinary town
to develop a chart might give us these headings:

Fire department
Police department
Animal control
City Hall
Civil Defense
County Court
Library
Parks
Water and sewer.

These headings are familiar from the list of subject headings in the reference and photo files, but they must be augmented by a listing of the offices found in City Hall, and a listing of boards and commissions.

When this chart or outline has been established, all materials collected from one office or agency are filed together consecutively, by office or origin, and by date. These groups of records are kept together. If offices of commissions change name or function, these changes are noted on the structure chart, the new name is used, but the record group continues as an entity.

Secondary divisions are grouped together under the primary heading of the department or commission. Series of like documents, such as planning office reports, are filed together by date, under agency, office, and type. Headings will ultimately look like this, depending entirely upon the function of the agency:

> *Mayor's office*
>
> Addresses, Proclamations, etc.
> Annual Reports
> Bulletins, Newsletters, etc.
> Constitutions, Charters, etc.
> Correspondence
> Manuals, Handbooks, etc.
> Maps
> Minutes of Meetings
> Periodicals
> Publications
> Press Releases
> Reports.

It will take a long time for these groupings to establish themselves, and not every agency will have every heading or type of document. Dates of the publication should appear on every item, because they are filed chronologically; this is the key to finding them within the file. The only exceptions

are continuations, parts, supplements, or amend-
ments, which are filed chronologically with the original publications.

Servicing these publications is a constant task.
Knowing what to collect, how to place each item
so that it is immediately available, and which item
or series of items a patron needs to answer a specific
question requires a depth of knowledge both about
the structure of the community and its agencies. This
awareness of current events is not acquired without
some work. When an important topic is under discussion in a locality, the collection should obtain
material on all aspects of the controversy. Perhaps
the reports of the planning commission are needed
by the public before another meeting of the commission, and then again before the commission reports
to the city council. The material provided to the
commission and the council as bearing on the decision is important to the public as well during this
period of study and discussion. When a decision has
been reached and implementation begins and publication of the report of the decision is achieved, the
bulk of the illustrative material is no longer needed.
It can be discarded, as now the minutes or published
reports of the hearings and meetings cover the subject.

The process of constantly eliminating material
from the current records group is the only weeding
ever done in a local history collection. When the
weeding (the elimination of duplicate, repetitive or
extraneous material) is completed, usually only
about ten percent of the bulk of the records remain.
The weeding should be done on a set schedule to
prevent accumulation of bulk. Material is usually
kept for a period of one to three years, and then
either discarded or placed into a permanent historical collection. A lateral file or standard file drawer
is the best equipment for storing this material.

The most important functions for a community
records collection are collecting and arranging the
material, providing quick service of it to the public,

and systematically weeding and sorting for the historical collection.

Community Resources

Sources other than local government can contribute to a community collection. Acquiring these materials may be more difficult than getting documents from the local governmental units, but it usually repays the effort. These items include the publications of the county, regional councils, and other such agencies. School records are valuable—discussions of school board policies, procedures, and curricula. Published reports of school districts and boards show a good deal about a community.

All such records should be sought on a regular basis and handled as are community records, using the agency or source as author. These records arranged chronologically. They must also be weeded constantly, selectively, and ruthlessly.

Collecting and servicing these materials, which is really a records management program, is an especially valuable contribution that a volunteer, or a group of volunteers, can make. Small teams can cover such areas as schools, churches, service organizations, and certain assigned offices on a regular basis, and do the weeding as necessary—subject to the review of the curator of the collection. When the immediacy of the situation has passed and some historical perspective has appeared, the materials can be reviewed and incorporated into the regular historical collection. The headings are built in.

When considering going into this kind of a collecting program, the responsibility for being open to serve the public is a factor. Once the materials are known to be available, people will want to use them. "Closed" signs make no friends for an institution. If an institution cannot properly serve the needs of the public and collection, the task is best left to the public official indicated by law or the public library. Just try to collect the documents as these institutions are through with them. Then the valuable ten percent can be added to the collection.

Collecting Current History

The present is the stuff of which history is made. Any institution intending to build a local history collection should be looking for items to answer questions both now and in the future. Much material of value can be acquired at no expense while it is current, as in a records program, if space is available to store it. The local newspaper, school, club and church newsletters, maps, photos which are donated—are all examples of easily acquired current materials.

Space is always a consideration in making collections, so current material must be evaluated just as is all other material. While a topic is current, several copies of the material may be needed; so may material illuminating several aspects of current questions, such as position papers and political speeches. When a situation has been resolved or a decision reached, much of the illustrative or interim material may be safely discarded, and only the best of multiple copies saved. As with records, only about ten percent of current material is worth keeping permanently. The rest has served its purpose during the discussion.

Save daily newspapers; they can be clipped for pertinent articles.

Indexing the local newspaper is the easiest way there is to control current history without adding bulk to the collection. The 3" x 5" or 4" x 6" card file, already established as a reference file, is perfectly adequate to keep the indexing under control. It uses the established subject headings, and notes newspaper, date and page number. This index is particularly useful when the newspaper is later microfilmed, but indexing is easier from a current newspaper in print. One staff member or volunteer should be assigned to do the indexing of the weekly or daily newspaper as it appears. He or she can do this at home, each time the paper appears, usually in less than an hour. Using the indexer's own news-

paper avoids mutilating the file copy by clipping.
It is a wonderful assignment for an elderly or shut-in
volunteer. Constant supervision must be exercised
by staff, however, to see that the indexing is kept
balanced, and does not simply reflect the indexer's
interests. Clippings may be pasted onto cards and
filed.

Except in articles of great local interest, it is not
necessary to index major daily newspapers from
metropolitan areas. They are usually indexed by the
publisher, and questions can be referred to the
newspaper library. Articles of special local interest
should be clipped and placed in the ephemera file,
carefully marked with source, date, and page.

Resource Persons

Another card list can be developed to help make
a local history collection the center for access to
community resources. This list notes persons in the
community who are able and willing to share their
expertise in local history. Access to persons who
have special knowledge, hobbies, skills, or interests
can enhance both collections and programs, and can
be a source of ready help to other organizations and
institutions. The organizations thus helped can be
expected to reciprocate by expanding the list and
by greater community participation. Also, it helps
make the local history center better known as the
custodian of local history. When the local history
collection is enhanced with resource persons plus
bibliographies, books, films, recordings, and other
audio and visual aids, the collection becomes the
point of origin for a great deal of educational and
cultural growth. It also tends to increase the base
of support the collection and its institution has in
the community.

By adding individuals or groups with interests and
expertise to share, this list can be used to develop
a speaker's bureau or an opinion survey. The list
of resource persons must be kept current, with the

knowledge and support of the persons listed. It should also contain a list of clubs and service agencies, churches, special events in the community, emergency services, and basic or important dates.

A very helpful outgrowth of this file or list could be a sheet or brochure to give to new residents, showing institutions, organizations, recreational and cultural facilities, as well as historical development.

For a local history or local affairs collection to be genuinely useful to an institution, it must reach out into the community beyond its usual constituency. Citizens must be made aware that they can find supporting and illustrative material for current topics in a historical context. They must be made aware of the services given and the research aids available. Films, resource persons, and special files must be made known. Publicity is not enough; it takes active participation and interest by a large number of citizens to make a local history collection. Special materials and special services are sometimes needed to reach new segments of the community; staff has to be constantly aware of local interests and activities. Cooperation among cultural groups and institutions, museums and libraries, schools and civic organizations can result in good for all concerned. Communication networks should be fostered; they improve service as well as reputation.

The local history collection, whether city, county or regional, whether located in a public library, a museum, or a local historical society, has a service to perform for its area. It may well become a nerve center for the entire community and should be a lively center of self-identification for the entire locale, both in the present and the future.

Appendix

Organizations

American Association for State and Local History
1400 Eighth Ave. South
Nashville, Tenn. 37203
   History News, technical leaflets, books on local history.

American Historical Association
400 A St. S.E.
Washington, D.C. 20003

American Library Association
50 E. Huron St.
Chicago, Ill. 60611
   American Libraries, Library Journal

R. R. Bowker Company
1180 Avenue of the Americas
New York, N.Y. 10036

Catholic Library Association
461 W. Lancaster Ave.
Haverford, Pa. 19041

National Microfilm Association
8728 Colesville Rd. Suite 1101
Silver Spring, Md. 20910

Oklahoma Library Association
801 W. Okmulgee
Muskogee, Ok. 74401

Organization of American Historians
112 N. Bryant St.
Bloomington, Ind. 47401

Pennsylvania Library Association
Room 506, 200 South Craig St.
Pittsburgh, Pa. 15213

Society of American Archivists
P.O. Box 8198
University of Illinois
Chicago, Ill. 60680

Special Library Association
235 Park Ave. South
New York, N.Y. 10003
   Special Libraries, Picturescope, Geography and Map Bulletin

H. W. Wilson Company
950 University Ave.
Bronx, New York, 10452
   Wilson Library Bulletin, Library Literature, Library Quarterly

Suppliers

Brodart Library Supplies
1609 Memorial Drive
Williamsport, Pa. 17701
and
15255 East Don Julian Road
City of Industry, Calif. 91749

Demco Library Supplies
Box 1488
Madison, Wis. 53701

Eastman Kodak Co.
343 State St.
Rochester, N.Y. 14650

Fisher Scientific Company
711 Forbes Ave.
Pittsburgh, Pa. 15219

Gaylord Library Supplies
155 Gifford St.
Syracuse, N.Y. 13201

Hollinger Corporation
3810 South Four Mile Run Drive
Arlington, Va. 22206
   acid-free paper, document boxes, photographic envelopes

Markilo Company
Capitol Station
Box 6452
Phoenix, Ariz. 85005
   quality plastic covers and envelopes

Process Materials Corporation
329 Veteran's Blvd.
Carlstadt, N.J. 07072
   conservation materials

TALAS
Technical Library Service
104 5th Ave.,
New York, N.Y. 10011
   conservation supplies, tools, and equipment.

University Paper Products, Inc.
Cabot St.
P.O. Box 101
Holyoke, Mass. 01040
  acid-free papers, boards

Publication Addresses

Ayer *Directory of Publications*
Ayer Press
210 W. Washington Square
Philadelphia, Pa. 19106
  entry by state and town, counties listed.

Journal of Librarianship
7 Ridgemount St.
London WCIE 7AE
England

Library Occurent
Indiana State Library
140 N. Senate Ave.
Indianapolis, Ind. 46204

Library Trends
Subscription Department
University of Illinois Press
Urbana, Ill. 61801

Manuscripts
The Manuscript Society
120 Prospect Ave.
Princeton, N.J. 08540

Newspapers In Microform, United States, 1948-1972
Library of Congress, Washington, D.C. 20540

Old Time New England
Society for the Preservation of New England Antiquities
14 Cambridge St.
Boston, Mass. 02114

Serials in Microform
Dissertations in Microform
Xerox, University Microfilm
Ann Arbor, Michigan 48106

Ulrich's International Periodicals Directory
R. R. Bowker Co.
1180 Avenue of the Americas
New York, N.Y. 10036
  18th ed. 1977 entry by subject.

Bibliography

General Works

Alderson, William T., Jr. "Securing Grant Support: Effective Planning and Preparation." AASLH Technical leaflet 62, 1972.

Anderson, Frank J. "A Sense of History; Some Notes on the Establishment and Maintenance of a Local History Collection in a Public Library." *Library Journal* 83:13 (July 1958) pp. 2003-2007.

Anderson, Linda. *Libraries for Small Museums.* Museum Brief no. 7. Columbia, Mo.: Museum of Anthropology, University of Missouri, 1971.

Bernhardt, G.H. "How to Organize and Operate a Small Library, Small Historical Museum or Local Historical Society." Fort Atkinson, Wis.: Highsmith, 1975.

Crittenden, Christopher. "The Public Library and Local Historical Sources." *History News* 30:7 (July 1975) pp. 69-70.

Dumke, Glenn S. "Digging History Out of Journalism, Mugbooks and Chambers of Commerce." *Wilson Library Bulletin* 33:4 (December 1958) pp. 277-281, 283.

Fridley, Russell W. "The Uses of Local History." AASLH Presidential Address, 1968.

Gregory, Lee H. "Local History and the Rural Library." *Library Journal* 81:1 (January 1, 1956) pp. 54-56.

Hobbs, John L. *Local History and the Library.* 2nd ed., completely revised and partly rewritten by George A. Carter. London: A. Duetsch, 1973.

Hoffman, A. "Preserving Historical Materials: Recovering a Region's Heritage." *Oklahoma Librarian* 22:10 (October 1972) pp. 7-8.

Hull, David, and Henry D. Fearnley. "The Museum Library in the United States." *Special Libraries* 67:7 (July 1976) p. 289.

Kaplan, Robin. "Art Bibliography." *Special Libraries* 64:3 (March 1973) p. 130.

Kaser, David. "The Library in the Small Historical Society." AASLH Technical leaflet 27, 1965.

Kujoth, Jean S., ed. *Readings in Nonbook Librarianship.* Metuchen, N.J.: Scarecrow Press, 1968.

Larsen, John C. "Art Reference Sources in Museum Libraries." *Special Libraries* 62:11 (November 1971) pp. 481-486.

Lipton, Barbara. "The Small Museum Library." *Special Libraries* 65:1 (January 1974) pp. 1-3.

Lord, Clifford L. *Student's Guides to Localized History.* New York: Teacher's College Press, Columbia University, 1965- .

Alabama	Cities:
Alaska	Boston
Arizona	Chicago
California	Cincinnati
Colorado	Denver
Connecticut	Houston
Delaware	Los Angeles
Florida	Miami
Georgia	Milwaukee
Hawaii	New York City
Idaho	Raleigh-Durham-Chapel Hill
Illinois	San Francisco
Kansas	Watersheds:
Kentucky	The Arkansas
Louisiana	The Canadian River Valley
Maryland	The Cimarron Valley
Massachusetts	The Delaware
Minnesota	The James
Mississippi	The Kansas
Missouri	The Kentucky
Montana	The Missouri Valley
Nebraska	The Ohio
New Hampshire	The Platte
New Jersey	The Potomac Valley
New Mexico	The Sacramento Valley
New York	The San Joaquin
North Carolina	The Snake
Ohio	The Susquehanna
Oklahoma	The Tennessee
Oregon	The Upper Missouri Valley
Pennsylvania	The Wisconsin Valley
Rhode Island	
South Dakota	Peoples:
Tennessee	The Finns
Texas	The Germans
Utah	The Greeks
Vermont	The Irish
Washington	The Italians
Wisconsin	The Mexicans
Wyoming	The Norwegians
	The Puerto Ricans
	The Swedes

Lord, Clifford. *Teaching History with Community Resources.* 2nd ed. New York: Teacher's College Press, Columbia University, 1965.

Lynes, A. *How to Organize a Local Collection.* London: A. Deutsch, 1974.

Martin, Bessie. "A Local History Collection in the Library." *Wilson Library Bulletin* 29:4 (December 1954) pp. 309-310, 312.

Matheson, William, "Approach to Special Collections." *American Libraries* 2:11 (December 1971) pp. 1151-1156.

Myrick, Shelby. "A Glossary of Legal Terminology." AASLH Technical leaflet 55, 1970.

New York State Education Department. *The Challenge of Local History: A Conference Designed to Broaden the Interests of New York State Local Historians in Scholarly History.* Albany: New York State Education Department, 1968.

Olson, James C. "The Role of Local History." AASLH Presidential Address, 1965.

Reed, M. "Local History Today: Current Themes and Problems for the Local History Library." *Journal of Librarianship* 7:3 (July 1975) pp. 161-181.

Russo, David J. *Families and Communities, A New View on American History.* Nashville: AASLH, 1974.

Sommer, Frank H. "A Large Museum Library." *Special Libraries* 65:3 (March 1974) pp. 99-103.

Stone, J. H., and J. W. Cortada. "Libraries and Local Historical Societies: The Need for Cooperation." *Journal of Library History* 6:4 (October 1971) pp. 360-364.

Suhler, Sam A. *Local History Collection and Services in a Small Public Library.* Pamphlet no. 19 of the Small Libraries Project, Library Administration Division. Chicago: American Library Association, 1970.

Thompson, Jean Beecher. "Local History in the Public Library." *Library Occurent* 21:4 (Spring 1968) pp. 103-109.

Tomlinson, Julette. "Local History in Legal Records." *Old Time New England* 58:4 (Spring 1968) pp. 103-109.

Walton, Clyde C., ed. "State and Local History in Libraries." *Library Trends* 13:2 (October 1964) pp. 153-272.

Microfilming

Avedon, Don M. "Standards: Microfilm Permanence and Archival Quality." *Special Libraries* 63:12 (December 1972) pp. 586-588.

Hale, Richard W. Jr., ed. *Guide to Photocopied Historical Materials in the U.S. and Canada.* Ithaca, N.Y.: American Historical Association, 1961.

Introduction to Micrographics. Silver Spring, Md.: National Microfilm Association, 1973.

Kiersky, Loretta. "New Developments in Photoreproduction." *Special Libraries* 60:9 (September 1969) pp. 434-436.

Sajor, Ladd Z. "Preservation Microfilming." *Special Libraries* 63:4 (April 1972) pp. 195-201.

Salmon, Stephen R. *Specifications for Library of Congress Microfilming.* Washington, D.C.: Library of Congress, 1964.

West, Donald G. "Film, the Durable Medium." *Special Libraries* 62:11 (November 1971) pp. 475-480.

Photographs and Prints

Bogan, Candace. "Architecture and Art Slide Collection." *Special Libraries* 66:12 (December 1975) p. 570.

Bowditch, George. "Cataloging Photographs." AASLH Technical leaflet 57, 1971.

Eaton, George T. "Preservation, Deterioration, Restoration of Photographic Images." *Library Quarterly* 40:1 (January 1970) pp. 85-98.

Faye, Helen. "May We Use This Picture?—Rights and Permissions." *Special Libraries* 56:1 (January 1965) pp. 23-26.

Fetros, John G. "Cooperative Picture Searching and Collection Development." *Special Libraries* 62:6 (June 1971) pp. 217-226.

Frankenburg, Celestine, and Romana Javitz. "Specialization: Pictures." *Special Libraries* 56:1 (January 1956) pp. 16-19.

Friedman, Barbara S. "The Oregon Historical Society Photograph Collection." *Picturescope* 19:3 (Fall 1971) pp. 135-144.

Hart, Arthur A. "Pictures and the Historical Society." *Picturescope* 19:3 (Fall 1971) pp. 133-135.

Keaveny, Sidney S. "Organizations Appealing to Picture Specialists." *Wilson Library Bulletin* 46:9 (May 1972) p. 834.

Keaveny, Sidney S. "Pictures." *Wilson Library Bulletin* 46:4 (February 1972) pp. 310-311.

Kodak Pamphlet No. J-19. "Black and White Processing for Permanence." Eastman Kodak Company, Rochester, N.Y. 14650. 54-3-73-AX.

Kusnerz, Peggy Ann, "Acquisition of Slides and Photographs: Results of a Survey of Colleges, Museums and Libraries." *Picturescope* 20:3 (Summer 1972) pp. 366-377.

Lothrop, E. S. Jr. "Books for the Collector of Old Photographs." *Picturescope* 19:2 (Summer 1971) p. 96.

Lothrop, E.S. Jr. "Care of Daguerreotypes and Ambrotypes: Advice from the Photographic Historical Society of New York." *Picturescope* 19:2 (Summer 1971) pp. 93-95.

Novotny, Ann, ed. *Picture Sources* 3. New York: Picture Division, Special Libraries Association, and American Society of Picture Professionals, 1975.

Ostroff, Eugene. "Conserving and Restoring Photographic Collections." Washington D.C.: American Association of Museums, 1976.

Rice, Stanley. "Picture Retrieval by Concept Coordination." *Special Libraries* 80:10 (December 1969) pp. 627-634.

Shaw, Renata V. "Picture Organization." *Special Libraries*, Part I, 63:10 (October 1972) p. 448. Part II, 63:11 (November 1972) p. 502.

Shaw, Renata V. "Picture Professionalism." *Special Libraries*, Part I, 65:10-11 (October-November 1974) p. 421. Part II, 65:12 (December 1974) p. 505.

Shaw, Renata V. "Picture Searching." *Special Libraries*, Part I, Techniques, 62:12 (December 1971) p. 524. Part II, Tools, 63:1 (January 1972) pp. 13-24.

Stewart, Milo V. "Organizing Your 2 x 2 Slides." AASLH Technical leaflet 88, 1976.

Tansey Luraine. "Classification of Research Photographs and Slides." *Library Trends* 23:3 (January 1975) pp. 417-426.

Weinstein, Robert A., and Larry Booth. *Collection, Use, and Care of Historical Photographs*. Nashville: AASLH, 1977.

Wilhelm, Henry. *Preservation of Contemporary Photographic Materials.* East Street Gallery, Box 616, Grinnell, Iowa 50112.

Zigrosser, Carl, and C. M. Gaehde. *A Guide to the Collecting and Care of Original Prints.* New York: Crown Publishers, 1965.

Oral History

American Library Association. *Recommendations for Audio-Visual Materials and Services for Small and Medium Sized Public Libraries.* Chicago: ALA, 1975.

Baum Willa K. *Oral History for the Local Historical Society.* Nashville: AASLH, 1974.

Baum, Willa K. *Transcribing and Editing Oral History.* Nashville: AASLH, 1977.

Catholic Library World, October, 1975. Entire issue devoted to oral history.

Fry, Amelia, and Willa Baum. "A Janus Look at Oral History." *American Archivist* 32:4 (October 1969) p. 319.

McNeil, William K. *Localizing Oral History.* Albany: New York State University, State Education Department, Office of Local History, 1969.

"Oral History: Some Questions to Ask." Society of American Archivists Committee on Oral History. *American Archivist* 36:3 (March 1973) p. 361.

Oral History Association. *Bibliography on Oral History.* Denton, Texas: The Association, 1975.

Oral History Association. *Colloquia on Oral History.* The Association, 1965-1971.

Oral History Association. Oral History Review 1973

Tyrrell, William G. "Tape Recording Local History." AASLH Technical leaflet 35, 1966.

Manuscripts and Archives

Anthony, Donald C. "Caring for Your Collections: Manuscripts and Related Materials." AASLH Technical leaflet 8, 1963.

Bordin, Ruth B. "Cataloging Manuscripts—A Simple Scheme." *American Archivist* 27:1 (January 1964) pp. 81-86.

Brubaker, Robert L. "Archival Principles and the Curator of Manuscripts." *American Archivist* 29:4 (October 1966) pp. 505-514.

Duckett, Kenneth W. *Modern Manuscripts.* Nashville: AASLH, 1975.

Gressley, Gene M. "Oil and History Do Mix." *Special Libraries* 61:10 (October 1970) pp. 433-440.

Kane, Lucille M. *Guide to the Care and Administration of Manuscripts.* Nashville: AASLH, 1966.

King, Richard L. "The Corporation as History." *Special Libraries* 60:4 (April 1969) pp. 203-206.

Lovett, Robert W. "Of Manuscripts and Libraries." *Special Libraries* 64:10 (October 1973) pp. 415-418.

Menzenska, Mary Jane. *Archives and Other Special Collections: A Library Handbook.* New York: School of Library Science, Columbia University, 1973.

Preston, Jean. "Problems in the Use of Manuscripts." *American Archivist* 28:3 (July 1965) pp. 367-379.

Smith, Russell M. "Stamping Manuscripts." *Manuscripts* 14:3 (1962) pp. 24-27.

Vail, R.W.G., ed. "Manuscripts and Archives." *Library Trends* 5:3 (January 1957) pp. 309-416.

Ephemera

Berner, Richard C. "On Ephemera: Their Collection and Use." *Library Resources* 7:4 (Fall 1963) pp. 335-339.

Berner, Richard C., and Gary M. Bettis. "Disposition of Non-manuscript Items Found Among Manuscripts." *American Archivist* 33:3 (July 1970) p. 275-281.

Dunn, Walter S., Jr. "Cataloging Ephemera: A Procedure for Small Libraries." AASLH Technical leaflet 58, 1972.

Ireland, Norma Olin. *A Pamphlet File in School, College and Public Libraries.* Westwood, Mass.: Faxon, 1954.

Lawrence, M. Therese. "What Access to Ephemera?" *Special Libraries* 64:7 (July 1973) pp. 285-290.

May, Ruby S. "Cataloging and Indexing Historical Collections." *Special Libraries* 66:4 (April 1975) pp. 217-222.

Webber, Olga. "Trimming the Clipping Files." *Special Libraries* 60:2 (February 1969) p. 82-86.

Maps and Measured Drawings

Brown, Lloyd A. "The Problem of Maps." *Library Trends* 13:2 (October 1964) pp. 215-225.

Capps, Marie T. "Preservation and Maintenance of Maps." *Special Libraries* 63:10 (October 1972) pp. 457-462.

Ehrenberg, Ralph. "Reproducing Maps in Libraries and Archives: The Custodian's Point of View"; and Charles G. LaHood. "The Photographer's Point of View." *Special Libraries* 64:1 (January 1973) pp. 18-19.

Galneder, Mary. "Equipment for Map Libraries." *Special Libraries* 61:7, 8 (July, August 1970) pp. 271-274.

Gerlach, Arch C. "Geography and Map Cataloging." *Special Libraries* 52:4 (May-June 1961) pp. 248-251.

Hebert, John J. "Panoramic Maps of American Cities." *Special Libraries* 63:12 (December 1972) pp. 554-562.

Johnson, Sheila G. "Geographic Arrangement of Topographic Maps." *Special Libraries* 68:3 (March 1977) pp. 115-118.

Kiraldi, Louis. "Courses in Map Librarianship." *Special Libraries* 61:9 (September 1970) pp. 496-500.

LeGear, Clara E. *Maps: Their Care, Repair and Preservation.* Washington, D.C.: Library of Congress, 1949.

Ristow, Walter W. "Map Librarianship." *Library Journal* 92:18 (October 15, 1967) pp. 3610-3614.

Smith, Richard D. "Maps, Their Deterioration and Preservation." *Special Libraries* 63:2 (February 1972) pp. 59-68.

Stephenson, Richard W. "Published Sources of Information About Maps and Atlases." *Special Libraries* 61:2 (February 1970) pp. 87-98.

Stevens, Stanley D. "Planning a Map Library? Create a Master Plan." *Special Libraries* 63:4 (April 1972) pp. 172-176.

Strain, Paula M. "Mountain Libraries, A Look at a Special Kind of Geographic Library." *Special Libraries* 64:11 (November 1973) pp. 483-489.

Western Association of Map Libraries. "Maps in the Local History Collection." *Information Bulletin* (June 1972) pp. 17-28.

White, Robert C. "Map Librarianship." *Special Libraries* 61:5 (May-June 1970) pp. 233-235.

Legal Questions

Connor, Seymour V. "A System of Manuscript Appraisal." AASLH Technical leaflet 41, 1967.

Kaiser, B. "Problems with Donors of Contemporary Collections." *American Archivist* 32:2 (February 1969) pp. 103-107.

MacBride, Dexter D. "Appraisals: of Objects in Historical Collections." AASLH Technical leaflet 97, 1977.

Newman, Ralph G. "Tax Problems of the Collector." AASLH Technical leaflet 31, 1965.

Rhoads, James B. "Alienation and Thievery: Archival Problems." *American Archivist* 29:2 (April 1966) pp. 197-208.

Society of American Archivists. *Forms Manual.* Chicago: Society of American Archivists, 1974.

Wickman, John E. "John Foster Dulles' Letter of Gift." *American Archivist* 31:4 (October 1968) pp. 355-363.

Winn, Karyl. "Common Law Copyright and the Archivist." *American Archivist* 37:3 (July 1974) pp. 375-386.

Technical Processes

Akers, Susan. *Simple Library Cataloging.* 5th ed. Metuchen, N.J.: Scarecrow Press, 1969.

Bartkowski, Patricia, and William Saffady. "Shelving and Office Furniture for Archives Buildings." *American Archivist* 37:1 (January 1974) p. 55.

Dearstyne, Bruce W. "Microfilming Historical Records." AASLH Technical leaflet 96, 1977.

Dunkin, Paul S. *How to Catalog a Rare Book.* 2nd ed. Chicago: American Library Association, 1972.

Hawken, William H. *Copying Methods Manual.* Chicago: American Library Association, Library Technology Project, no. 11, 1966.

Jesse, William H. *Shelf Work in Libraries.* Chicago: American Library Association, 1952.

Manning, Anita. "Data Retrieval Without a Computer." AASLH Technical leaflet 85, 1975.

Osborn, Andrew D. *Serial Publications.* Chicago: American Library Association, 1955.

Reprographic Services in Libraries: Organization and Administration. Chicago: American Library Association, Library Technology Project, no. 19, 1969.

Services

Hale, Richard W., Jr. "Methods of Research for the Amateur Historian." AASLH Technical leaflet 21, 1969.

Jones, William K. "The Exhibit of Documents." AASLH Technical leaflet 75, 1974.

Miller, Carolyn L. "Genealogical Research." AASLH Technical leaflet 14, revised 1969.

Warner, Sam Bass. "Use of Social Statistics." AASLH Technical leaflet 17, 1963.

Wilson, Don W., and Dennis Medina. "Exhibit Labels: A Consideration of Content." AASLH Technical leaflet 60, 1972.

Conservation

Barrow, William J. Manuscripts and Documents: Their Deterioration and Restoration. 2nd ed. Charlottesville: University Press of Virginia, 1972.

Clapp, Ann F. Curatorial Care of Works of Art on Paper. 2nd revised ed. Oberlin, Ohio: Intermuseum Conservation Association, 1974.

Cunha, George M. "Conserving Local Archival Materials on a Limited Budget." AASLH Technical leaflet 86, 1975.

Cunha, George M. "National Trends in Cooperative Approaches to Conservation." Pennsylvania Library Association Bulletin 28:6 (November 1973) p. 226.

Cunha, George M., and Dorothy G. Cunha. Conservation of Library Materials: A Manual and Bibliography of the Care, Repair and Restoration of Library Materials. 2 vol. 2nd ed., revised. Metuchen, N.J.: Scarecrow Press, 1971-1972.

Doms, Keith, ed. "Preservation of Library Materials". Pennsylvania Library Association Bulletin 28:6 (November 1973) pp. 219-251. Reprinted as a pamphlet.

Friedman, Hannah B. "Preservation of Library Materials: State of the Art." Special Libraries 59:10 (October 1968) pp. 608-613.

Friedman, Hannah B. "Preservation Programs in New York State." Special Libraries 60:11 (November 1969) pp. 578-589.

Friedman, Hannah B., and Wayne Eley, comp. Conservation of Library Materials: A Suggested Reading List. New York: New York Public Library, 1973.

Guldbeck, Per E. The Care of Historical Collections. Nashville: AASLH, 1972.

Hall, David. "Phonorecord Preservation." Special Libraries 62:9 (September 1971) pp. 357-362.

King Antoinette. "Conservation of Drawings and Prints." Special Libraries 63:3 (March 1972) pp. 116-120.

Lydenberg, H. M., J. Archer, and J. Alden. The Care and Repair of Books. New York: R. R. Bowker, 1960.

Minogue, Adelaide E. The Repair and Preservation of Records. Washington, D.C.: National Archives, 1960.

Protecting the Library and its Resources. Chicago: American Library Association, Library Technology Project no. 7, 1963.

Rachow, Louis A. "Care and Preservation of Theatre Library Materials." *Special Libraries* 63:1 (January 1972) pp. 25-30.

Rath, Frederick L., and Merrilyn O'Connell. *A Bibliography on Historical Organization Practices: Care and Conservation of Collections.* Nashville: AASLH, 1977.

Santen, Vernon, and Howard Crocker. "Historical Society Records: Guidelines for a Protection Program." AASLH Technical leaflet 18, 1972.

Tribolet, Harold. "Rare Book and Paper Repair Techniques." AASLH Technical leaflet 13, revised 1970.

Theory and Practice of Bookbinding. United States Training Series, Government Printing Office. Washington D.C.: Government Printing Office, 1962.

Wagner, Robert W. "Motion Picture Restoration." *American Archivist* 32:2 (April 1969) pp. 125-132.

Waters, Peter. *Procedures for Salvage of Water-Damaged Library Materials.* Washington D.C.: Library of Congress, 1975.

Wilson, W. K., and J. L. Gear. *Care of Books, Documents, Prints, and Films.* National Bureau of Standards Consumer Information Series no. 5. Washington D.C.: Government Printing Office, 1971.

Winger, H., and R. Smith, eds. *Deterioration and Preservation of Library Materials.* Chicago: University of Chicago Press, 1970.

Training of Staff and Volunteers

Alderson, William T., and Shirley Payne Low. *Interpretation of Historic Sites.* Nashville: AASLH, 1976.

Bradshaw, Mary Claire. "Volunteer Docent Programs: A Pragmatic Approach to Museum Interpretation." AASLH Technical leaflet 65, 1973.

Davis, Elinor, and Lee-Allison Levene. "Workshop Strategy: A Survival Guide for Planners. *Special Libraries* 66:2 (February 1975) pp. 85-91.

Hasenbein, Sister F. "Care and Time Given to Volunteers Pay Off." *Catholic Library World* 44:8 (April 1973) pp. 531-535.

Menzenska, Mary Jane. *Archives and Other Special Collections: A Library Staff Handbook.* New York: School of Library Science, Columbia University, 1973.

Montgomery, Florence M. "Training of Guides." AASLH Technical leaflet 18, 1964.

Offerman, Sister M. C. "Workshop for Library Volunteers," *Catholic Library World* 44:8 (April 1973) pp. 536-539.

"Volunteers in Libraries: An Untapped Asset?" *Library Journal* 96:10 (September 1971) pp. 2717-2718.

Community Records

Hungerford, Anthos F. "United States Government Publications: Acquisitions Procedures for the Small Library." *Special Libraries* 65:1 (January 1974) pp. 22-25.

Jones, Mary Ellen. "Photographing Tombstones." AASLH Technical leaflet 92, 1977.

Jordan, Philip D. "In Search of Local Legal Records." *American Archivist* 33:4 (October 1970) pp. 379-382.

Newman, John J. "Cemetery Transcribing: Preparations and Procedures." AASLH Technical leaflet 9, revised 1971.

Scarich, K., and M. Trumpeter. "Community Information Inventory: Dope that Users Can't Find." *Wilson Library Bulletin* 46:3 (November 1971) pp. 256-259.

Index